Foreword

As an avid fisherman for over 35 years I understand the importance of maintaining a reel to perform at its best during any situation. Would you go into battle without a properly maintained and functioning weapon? No, of course not, and in the world of fishing, your reel is your weapon. Over the course of almost four decades I have seen many anglers become frustrated, angry or worse lose the fish of their dreams because of a poorly maintained reel. Sounds simple, but time and time again anglers neglect one of the key components in their arsenal of equipment, their reels.

Every angler, whether a beginner or highly experienced tournament angler, should know how to service their reels, no differently than every solider has to know how to service their weapons. How many times have we all said at one time or another, "If you want something done right you have to do it yourself"?

In this book I teach you everything you need to know about your reels, from what it's made of, what the best products are to use, to step by step maintenance photos from experts around the world. Never has such a comprehensive book been made available to anglers, these are the secrets that reel repair centers have closely guarded for many years.

In the past, anglers were not as in-tuned to maintaining their reels as they are today, with more technological advances also comes more precise and more sensitive gear to the weather and elements. However, anglers sometimes think that as long as the reel is not dropped in the sand, water, or dirt that it should not need as much periodic maintenance, however consider the case of the surf fishermen, the reel is subjected to windblown sands, roasting sunlight, and saltwater spray, all without even touching the ground.

In this book I give you the knowledge you need to properly care for and maintain fishing reels for years of enjoyment and operating at peak performance for when it really counts! No more spending hard earned cash paying someone else to do your reel maintenance, or waiting days or weeks to get your reel back. You can do all this from the comfort of your own home.

I cover a lot of topics within the book, simply because there are a lot of outside influences when it comes to reels, including lines, lubricants, reel covers, and a lot more that all affect the performance, serviceability and sustainability of any reel. I hope that you will refer to the book often and that it will become a valuable addition to your reference library.

Jeff Holder

"Very comprehensive and easy to read, a book every angler should have in their reference library. It inspires me to tune up my reels" -
Rob Faddis, President, RMR Industries

"This is the single best resource for anyone doing any kind of reel repair or service" -
Jason Flanzbaum, VP, Boca Bearings

Fishing Reel Care and Maintenance 101

"Fight the Fish...Not the Reel"

Piscator Publishing – Los Angeles, California
2009

©Copyright 2009 Jeff Holder. Printed and bound in the United States of America. All rights reserved. No part of this book may be reproduced or transmitted in any form or by any means, electronic or mechanical, including photocopying, recording, or by an information storage and retrieval system – with the exception of a reviewer who may quote brief passages in a review to be printed in a newspaper or magazine – without written permission from the publisher or author. For information contact jeff@reelschematic.com

This book includes information from many sources and gathered from many personal experiences. It is published for general reference and is not intended to be substitute for independent verification by readers when necessary and appropriate. The book is sold with the understanding that neither the author nor the publisher is engaged in rendering financial or legal advice. The publisher and author disclaim any personal liability, directly or indirectly, for advice or information presented within. Although the author and publisher have prepared this manuscript with utmost care and diligence and have made every effort to ensure the accuracy and completeness of the information contained within, we assume no responsibility for errors, inaccuracies, omissions, or inconsistencies.

Includes index.

ISBN:	144860897X
EAN-13:	9781448608973

DEDICATION

This book is dedicated to my children
Haley, Candice, Cassie and Aaron
May god be with you and guide you throughout
your life and protect you always. Always be
true to yourself and who you are.

And to my wife Kathleen for who none of this
would have been possible without her undying
support for all my dreams.

Table of Contents

HISTORY OF THE FISHING REEL	1
CHOOSING A REEL	8
BREAK IT DOWN	13
MATERIALS USED IN REEL CONSTRUCTION	14
ALUMINUM	
GRAPHITE AND PLASTICS	
MAGNESIUM	
BUSHINGS AND BEARINGS	21
TYPICAL DRAG SYSTEM	30
FISHING REEL CARE AND MAINTENANCE	33
TIPS FOR PROTECTING REELS	
BASIC CLEANING TIPS	
BASIC TOOLS	
LUBRICATION	
BAITCASTING LUBRICATION POINTS	
SPINNING REEL LUBRICATION POINTS	
SHIMANO TRINIDAD\TORIUM DRAG UPGRADE	49
DAIWA SALTIST 30H (40&50)	80
PENN 500, 501, JIGMASTER	112
DAIWA FUEGO REEL BREAKDOWN	147
FISHING LINE	158
TYPES OF FISHING LINE	
PROPERTIES OF LINE	
THE PROPER CARE OF LINE	
LURE AND LINE CONDITIONERS	
CRYOGENIC TREATMENT OF REELS, LINE AND RODS	193
THINGS YOU SHOULD KNOW	200
IS YOUR BOAT PROTECTED	202
REEL SERVICE AND PARTS SUPPLY DIRECTORY	204

REEL WARRANTY SERVICE 207
    ABU-GARICA REELS 207
    ACCURATE REELS 209
    AVET REELS 211
    DAIWA REELS 213
    FIN-NOR REELS 215
    HARDY REELS 217
    OKUMA REELS 218
    PINNACLE REELS 219
    PENN REELS 221
    QUANTUM REELS 223
    SHAKESPEARE REELS 226
    SHIMANO REELS 228
    ZEBCO REELS 229
INDEX 231

History of the Fishing Reel

Historians have long been frustrated with trying to trace the origin of the fishing reel. There have been several differing points of views, each with its own reasons.

In 1651, English literature first wrote about a "wind" installed within two feet of the lower end of the rod. This has been usually accepted as the earliest known written reference to a reel. However, there are examples of Oriental paintings that depict Chinese fishermen using reels that date to the twelfth century. One of the most famous is entitled "Angler on a Wintry Lake", by Ma Yuan, c1195. Another fishing reel was featured in a painting by Wu Zhen (1280–1354). The book *Tianzhu lingqian* (Holy Lections from Indian Sources), printed sometime between 1208 and 1224, features two different woodblock print illustrations of fishing reels being used. An Armenian parchment Gospel of the 13th century shows a reel (though not as clearly depicted as the Chinese ones). The *Sancai Tuhui*, a Chinese

encyclopedia published in 1609, features the next known picture of a fishing reel and vividly shows the windlass pulley of the device.

The earliest reels were used primarily as a storage device for line, where line could be wound or pulled off. Each turn of the handle was a single rotation of the spool, 1:1 ratio.

There has been much debate about when the first multiplier reel arrived. One theory is that the first modern era reels were made in Britain. The other is that George Snyder of Kentucky built the earliest "multiplier reel" in the 1820's. The key advance of this reel was the mechanical action; each turn of the handle produced four turns of the spool. George Snyder was actually a watch maker by trade, and made a few of the reels for him and friends. These reels became the basis of the "Kentucky Reels", made by Meek, Milam, Sage, Hardman, and Gayle. Most of who were trained as jewelers and had experience cutting gears and precision lathe work. Copies of the hand-made reels were soon available from mass production lines from major producers at a fraction of the cost of hand-made. This stimulated the sale of multiplying reels and increased their popularity.

However, in speaking with antique reel expert Tom Greene, most of what we could recognize as fishing reels today seem to have started in England back in the mid-17th century. At first the reel was nothing more than a way to retrieve extra line that would otherwise be wrapped by hand or left to lie on the floor of a vessel or in the sand at an angler's feet. And as far as today's ultra-accurate, fine-tuning drag goes, it just didn't exist.

Hard to believe, but it's true. As a matter of fact, many early modern models (those created during the late 1700's and early 1800's) were what are called direct-drive reels. In other words, if you turned the handle of these usually silver- or brass-bodied weighty reels, line would come in. One turn of the handle would make one turn of the likely cork-made spool, and, without a drag system or antireverse mechanism, if line was taken off the reel when a fish went running for the horizon, the handle would spin backwards. A back-spinning reel must've appeared a blur if a sizable game fish such as a tarpon, tuna, or marlin was on the line of one of these early models. The failed results of early anglers could be measured in the number of knuckles they busted during their fishing career.

Before the introduction of a counterbalance ball, three-handled reels like this one enhanced an angler's ability to cast

In spite of these challenges, there were intrepid and pioneering fishermen like Charles Frederick Holder, who happily chased tarpon in Florida and then moved to California to discover massive bluefin tuna just off the coast of Catalina. Luckily, by the time Holder made his way west in the late 1800's (he caught the first-known bluefin tuna on rod and reel, a hefty 183-pounder in 1897), a couple of drag systems were available, although some anglers were hesitant to embrace the new technology. A famous early reel builder named James Vom Hofe had one of the first-known star-drag systems on the body of a fishing reel, on which turning a star-shape mechanism applied side pressure to the spool, slowing down the exit of the line. The star drag is still used today, but it's hard to measure how much resistance is being put on the line with such a system, and it can therefore easily overcome a line's breaking strength.

Holder, though aware of this new technology, used the more easily understood technology of the time: a leather thumb pad, which allowed an angler to use his finger to push down on the line and gauge by feel how much pressure was being applied. The heat buildup must've been significant for the likes of Holder, especially when spending nearly five hours besting his first tuna. Early anglers also had to fight the fact that they were dealing with reels that were hard-mounted to the rod from which they were fished. Some reels were simply tied to rods, some were clamped, and others screwed and/or bolted. It was crude, but it was a start. It would be many decades before the idea of adjustable mounts on rods and sturdy reel seats would become standard issue. Other advancements—such as lightweight fiberglass rods and lightweight reels with cast-aluminum bodies and machined stainless steel gears—provide an angling edge to today's fishermen. The days of heavy silver and brass are gone.

The concept of multiplying gears, which had its origins in England around 1750, made its way into many reels, too. This technology allowed an angler to turn the handle on a reel and get more than one revolution of line on the spool, a great advancement over the direct-drive predecessors. These early multipliers allowed for a retrieval rate of about 3:1; today that rate can be as much as 6:1.

But not everything new is necessarily better. For instance, Greene commented that the early reel builders such as J.F. and B.F. Meek handcrafted their product to such exacting tolerances that the screws on the sideplates of the reel were numbered to fit into specific holes. (The Meeks constructed a custom reel for President Grover Cleveland, which currently resides in the Smithsonian.) These reels had a true custom feel and often sported decorative engravings, too.

Take note of this early casting reel's cork spool and level-wind feature.

The Meeks also realized reel balance was important for casting anglers. The older single-handle reel initially didn't cast well, so the Meeks made a three-handle model that was balanced for easy casting. Soon after, advancements in reel counterbalance eventually led to the ball-handle reel dubbed the New York: a ball of silver attached to one side of the handle whose counterweight allowed for an even freespool throw.

In addition, unlike today's often aircraft-grade ball bearings, which help make the guts of a reel run smoothly, pioneer builders like Edward Vom Hofe used actual jewels such as agate for bearings on baitcasters. (Some early builders had a background in working with jewels). Not surprising, early reels weren't cheap, either. A baitcaster back in the 1870's could run upwards of $22, which would amount to a few to several hundred dollars today.

But improved production methods, ball bearings, and more affordable raw materials would eventually bring reels to the masses. For instance, Penn Reels, one of fishing's premier reel manufacturers for more than 70 years, began mass-manufacturing its reels in 1933. And at the time one of its star-drag reels cost about $2.50.

This triple-handle model is from custom makers J.F. and B.F. Meek, who also produced a reel for President Grover Cleveland.

(Today some of Penn's star-drag Senator Reels can be purchased for around $110 to $300, depending on the model, and its International Baitcasters run from about $200 to $300.

William C. Boschen, a member of the Catalina Tuna Club of California, is credited with the original concept for the first internal star drag reel. A prototype was made in Brooklyn, New York by reel manufacturer Julius Vom Hofe, and used by Boschen to catch the first broadbill swordfish (358 pounds) ever taken on a sporting rod and reel. The catch was in the summer of 1913 off Catalina Island. However, it's Penn Reels that gets credited with improving on the star drags and developing the fine-tuned, lever-drag system that is the backbone of many solidly performing big-game reels today. Nowadays top manufacturers from Alutecnos to Shimano, Accurate to Avet, and more, all offer the exactness of a lever drag.

Because of this original concept by William C. Boschen of the Catalina Tuna Club, all reels today classified as conventional and baitcasting have star drag designs.

Choosing a Reel

There are thousands of different reels on the market so how do you decide which reel is right for you? To simplify the process of selecting a reel you should first concentrate on the main features and components that make each reel different. Then evaluate what your specific fishing needs are, by combining this and the knowledge of reel features you will be able to make a better informed decision.

Ask yourself these questions:
1) What type of fish will you be catching?
2) What will be the average size of these fish?
3) What pound test line will you be using?
4) Will you be casting, trolling or bottom fishing?

This will give you a general idea of the requirements your reel needs to meet, and will narrow down your search. Purchasing a reel with less than you need leads to many unsatisfactory trips, the same holds true for purchasing a reel that has too many features for what you need.

CATEGORY

Which category would best fit your needs? Closed Face Spinning Reels, Open Faced Spinning Reels, Conventional, Bait Casting Reels or Fly Reel. If you are a novice, or first timer you might consider the closed face spinning reel since the experience needed is minimal and operation is very easy, backlash is also essentially a non-issue. Or you might want to step up to an open faced spinning reel if you have a little more experience. If you are an experienced angler then the bait casting reel would probably suit you best since this will allow you to maximize your casting distance and overall performance. If you are saltwater fishing, often the conventional reel setup is best.

DRAG SYSTEMS

When you are buying either a conventional or bait casting reel you can choose to get either a star drag or a lever drag system. Star drags are adjusted by turning the star shaped gear behind the handle. Lever drags are simple to use, smoother, provide a more consistent performance and allow for adjustments in more precise increments, however the price is usually more for these drag systems.

BALL BEARINGS

When it comes to smooth performance and durability, sealed stainless steel bearings are preferred over bushings. In general terms, the more ball bearings a reel has the more smoothly it will operate. In newer models you will typically see between 8 and 12 ball bearings.

GEAR RATIO

This refers to how many revolutions the spool makes with each turn of the handle, for example a ratio of 3:1 means for every 1 turn of the handle the spool turns 3 times. Lower gear ratios are normally used with baits such as crank baits when you want a slower retrieve speed and heavy cranking power. Faster gear ratios are used for spinner baits, or when you want to gain line in a hurry such as when the fish charges you. If you are purchasing a conventional reel then you are in luck because with two-speed models you get the best of both worlds, High-gear for faster retrieves and Low-gear for more powerful cranking, all at the touch or pull of a button.

HOUSINGS AND FRAMES

Most reels are made of either aluminum (die-cast or forged) or graphite; both materials have advantages and disadvantages. Reels made of anodized aluminum are stronger and more durable, but they are heavier. Graphite on the other hand is both light and corrosion resistant but not as strong. Most conventional reels today are machined from a solid piece of stock, and manufacturers have even started using one-piece graphite bodies as well.

CASTING CONTROLS

Both conventional and bait casting reel usually come with some special built in casting control systems, these can be either centrifugal or magnetic and either internally or externally adjustable. These are meant to help prevent backlash, but even with all these controls nothing replaces an educated thumb that comes with experience.

LEVEL WIND MECHANISMS

Baitcasters and some conventional reels feature a level wind which ensures that as the line is retrieved it is distributed evenly on the spool. This is a great convenience however they do tend to have more mechanical difficulties. A level wind also will slightly reduce your casting distance because of the extra opening the line has to travel through.

SPOOLS

Spools are normally made of either graphite or anodized aluminum, depending on the type of fishing you will be doing will depend on which spool design will be best. Anodized aluminum spools offer greater strength and durability, but with a less free spool rate than a graphite spool. For large fish, which can create a great deal of torque you should use an anodized aluminum spool, for average freshwater fishing a graphite spool may pertain more since you want to focus on casting distance and smaller weight fish will not create excessive torque on the spool. There are also chromed, bronze or stainless steel spools offered on some reels, metal spools like these are best for heady duty fishing or when using specialized lines like Dacron or wire.

GEAR RATIO AND LINE RECOVERY

No matter what a reel's gear ratio, the evaluation of the ability of the reel to retrieve line is called

"Inches Per Turn (IPT)". This is the amount of line retrieved per turn of the handle. This is determined by both the gear ratio and the diameter of the spool (this is also slightly dependant on the amount of line on the spool).

This is what the angler should be concerned with when purchasing a reel, however this is hard to calculate because manufacturers seldom display the spool diameter on the box.

CALCULATING LINE RETRIEVAL LENGTH WITH GEAR RATIO

You can calculate how much line is retrieved for any given gear ratio with this formula:
Average Spool Diameter x 3.14 x ratio = length of line per one turn of the handle
For example with a 30mm spool diameter and 5.5:1 gear ratio
30mm x 3.14 x 5.5 = 518.1 mm of line or about 20.3 inches

Spool Diameter (Inches)	4.4:1 gear ratio	5.1:1 gear ratio	6.2:1 gear ratio
1.25	5.39	6.25	7.60
1.50	7.77	9.01	10.95
1.75	10.58	12.26	14.91
2.00	13.82	16.01	19.47
2.25	17.49	20.27	24.65
2.50	21.59	25.03	30.42
2.75	26.13	30.28	36.82
3.00	31.09	36.04	43.82
3.25	36.49	42.30	51.42
3.50	42.33	49.06	59.65
3.75	48.59	56.32	68.47
4.00	55.29	64.08	77.90

Break It Down!

Reels are basically line management devices, capable of line storage, line retrieval, and line dispensing. But what materials are used in the production of reels? This is especially useful information when you are selecting cleaning agents for metal, fiber and plastic parts.

Materials Used in Reel Construction

Why is it so important to know the materials used in the construction of the reels you are maintaining? Simple, it will determine the cleaning and lubricating products that you should use, and their expected lifetimes. When it comes to the metals that reels are made of it varies depending on the cost and engineering requirements, the range can be from simple die cast alloys (aluminum and zinc) through machinable, tough aerospace alloys (hardened high tensile strength aluminum).

As a basic rule of thumb, metals are generally stronger than polymers. This is the reason, that the internal gears of reels are almost always metals, such as brass, stainless steel, aluminum bronze and other alloys. In high-end reels the body is usually machined from a solid block or billet of metal, which results in the strongest possible structure.

Another reason for using metals is because of their rigidity which allows them to maintain precise alignment even when subject to heavy stress. A misalignment can result in power loss and gear wear.

Weight, corrosion, and lack of shock resistance are the negative aspects of using metals in reel construction. Aluminum comprises the bulk of metal used in reel fabrication because of it light weight compared to stainless steel, brass, or steel. Titanium which is extremely lightweight is still presently too expensive and too hard to machine to be practical for reel manufacturing but in the future we may see this change and become main stream in reel fabrication.

Metals can be surface treated to inhibit corrosion; this is done through a process known as anodizing. Anodizing is an electrochemical coating process which can be both tough and colorful, as nearly any color can be dyed into the coating. Almost all top end reels with golden or flat black finishes use dyed anodized coatings for protection. Some reel manufacturers go even one step farther and have started anodizing internal metal parts to further protect against saltwater corrosion.

Graphite Mesh

Graphite and Plastics

Polymer, sometimes called graphite, reel bodies are injection molded. The polymers include ABS, nylons, and similar materials, and the fibers that strengthen it are chopped fiberglass, graphite (Figure 1) and silicon carbide. Don't confuse with word plastics with "cheap" like a kids toy might be, plastics are used in modern firearms for example, and can withstand enormous loads.

What makes plastic so great is their production economy, light weight and corrosion resistance. The cost of production is extremely low compared to metal production.

The fabrication temperature is at a lower temperature and the die-casts last a lot longer, which both result in a lower product cost for the angler.

Plastics are inherently resistant to corrosion and usually do not require any finishing because colored fibers can be added to the polymer before molding.

The negative aspects include distortion and wear. Distortion results because polymers have to maintain a degree of flexibility to avoid any brittleness, especially at low temperatures. An overly rigid polymer can result in a crack, called crack propagation. The whole purpose of the strength fibers is to limit crack propagation. Flexibility is not a total negative aspect however, because of its flexibility polymers offer excellent shock resistance, giving the reel a better chance of surviving a hard fall than its metal counterpart.

For both metal and polymer bodied reels, most of the negative aspects can be avoided through regular maintenance. Usually, the potentially bad aspects of a product are exacerbated through neglect, and the reel is perfectly capable of delivering good service and value whether made of metal or plastics.

Daiwa Fuego (Fire)
© Photo courtesy of Daiwa Corporation

Magnesium

As angler's we are constantly obsessed with weight, and are driving manufacturers to provide lighter equipment, and the reel has been no exception to this. Today manufacturers lean towards Magnesium frames to provide the lightest reels on the market. Magnesium allows manufacturers to produce a frame that is lighter than aluminum, offers exceptional part density and surface quality that cannot be matched by plastic. The other advantage is the ability to create complex geometry

Shimano Chronarch MG50
© Photo courtesy of Shimano

with varying wall thickness, while maintaining tight tolerances of bores and surfaces for mating components.

Some examples of reels that use magnesium frames are Daiwa Steez, Daiwa Pro Team Fuego (Figure 2), Pflueger Supreme, Shimano Chronarch MG50, and many other brands/models.

Now this might get you to thinking, isn't Magnesium highly corrosive? Yes, without a special protectant. Which is why manufacturers recommend that you do not use magnesium based reels in saltwater conditions unless they have been specially treated with a protectant, such as Shimano does to its Chronarch MG50 reel.

This was from a 2005 article about Phillips Plastics Corp. - Phillips Plastics Corporation recently won an International Die Casting Competition award from the North American Die Casting Association (NADCA) for the manufacture of a fishing reel frame developed by Marsh Technologies, Inc. This award was received for the "under 0.5 pounds" category.

According to NADCA's press release, "Weighing less than 31 grams, the reel (frame) was lighter than aluminum and offered exceptional part density and surface quality that could not be matched by plastic. Other advantages noted by the judges included the ability to create complex geometry with varying wall thickness, while maintaining tight tolerances of bores and surfaces for mating components."

"The entries in the 2005 competition prove that North American die casters are continuing to push the frontiers for parts that improve finished products, reduce assembly time, and contribute to the overall success of manufacturers," adds Daniel Twarog, NADCA President. "A great deal of this success is the result of die casters and manufacturers working as partners to develop effective solutions."

Why Use Different Metals?

In conventional reels the main drive gear and the pinion gear are always made of different metals, one metal is always softer than the other. Most have a stainless steel pinion gear and a bronze main gear; there are several reasons for this, same materials tend to cold weld or "gall" together, while dissimilar metals offer lower coefficient of friction. Also two materials of the same hardness would amplify any imperfections in the machining of the gears, and any piece of sand/grit that might get on the teeth.

In the best of situations the main drive gear will be of slightly softer metal than the pinion gear, for wear purposes. The best way to think of this is, in a 6:1 gear ratio, the pinion gear teeth are struck 6 times more than the teeth on the main drive gear, and hence the pinion gear needs to be made of stronger metal because of the increased wear.

In almost all better quality reels you will find the gears are helically milled, this means that each gear tooth is curved, rather than straight. Helical milling results in greater strength, thicker cross section, and a high degree of smoothness. One of the biggest benefits over straight teeth is that it allows several teeth to at least be partially engaged at all times, thus spreading the load and stress out, where in straight teeth only one tooth at a time is engaged.

Bushings and Ball Bearings

The basic task of bushings and ball bearings is to precisely support a rotating shaft with minimum friction. In revolving-spool reels and fixed-spool reels, a rotating shaft supports the handle and gear train, which the angler cranks for retrieve; in revolving-spool reels, the rotating shaft also supports the spool, and in fixed-spool reels, it also supports the rotor.

Bushings

A bushing, sometimes called a sleeve bearing, supports the rotating shaft with a smoothly finished hole and a lubricating film. The bushing material can be the same as that of the reel body itself but is typically a distinctly separate material for better wear and lower friction. The physical contact between bushing and shaft is subject to sliding of one surface over the other, so there's a need for smooth mechanical finishing and lubrication.

For relatively low loads, the body material of diecast reels is a suitable bushing material. The common diecast metal is Zamak, a zince/aluminum alloy with good machining characteristics. Its coefficient of friction with a steel shaft (a measure of the amount of friction between the metals) is low, and a lubricating film makes it even lower. The lubricating film is required to keep the surfaces from actually touching, and must not only withstand the pressure of the contact, but retain this property at higher temperatures as well.

Bushing materials which differ from that of the reel body are used for greater loads and include such metals as brass and bronze, as well as fiber-reinforced polymers, These bushings are firmly installed with a press fit, or cven adhesives, because inadvertent rotation of the bushing would disastrously wear an oversized hole in the reel body. The bushing materials are selected to optimize mechanical properties, such as abrasion resistance and low friction. The metals are often sintered from granules and the resultant porous structure allows either storage or free passage of lubricants, which extends service life for the bushing. Other alloys contain graphite flakes which "self-lubricate" the bushings. Polymer bushings are strengthened with chopped fibers in the matrix. A well-made bushing gives extremely smooth rotation for the operation of the fishing reel.

Ball Bearings

One major advantage of ball bearings over bushings is under heavy load conditions. Under low load conditions, the difference between the two systems  is virtually indistinguishable, but as the load on the shaft increases, the superior performance of the ball bearing becomes increasingly apparent. Ball bearings support their load through a rolling action in

Fishing Reel Care and Maintenance 101 | 23

contrast to the sliding action of the bushing. The difference can be compared to moving a rock on wheels versus dragging it along the ground; the heavier the rock, the more apparent the difference between the two methods.

Standard material for rings and balls is a vacuum degassed high carbon chromium steel allowing for high efficiency, low torque, low noise level and long bearing life. For bearings requiring anti-corrosion or heat-resistance properties, marensitic stainless steel is used.

- Avet and Accurate bearings are both sealed bearings, meaning they have a side plate that is usually either blue or black made of phosphor bronze and plastic laminate that is pressed in.

Bearing Characteristics	*courtesy of Boca Bearings
Load	Single row radial ball bearings with ball separated by a cage can support radial loads, axial loads and tilting movements. All full complement V-type ball bearing can support only radial loads and some low axial loads.
Speed	Maximum permissible speeds for ball bearings are mainly related to the bearing design and size, cage type, bearing internal clearance, the method and type of lubrication, manufacturing accuracy, sealing methods and loads.
Torque & Noise Levels	Single row radial ball bearings are precision components and have low torque and noise levels.
Inclination of Inner/Outer Rings	Shaft and housing seats with poor accuracy, fitting errors and shaft bending might cause inclination between the inner and outer rings, although the internal clearance of the bearing will permit this to a certain extent. Generally, the maximum permissible inclination between the inner and out rings is approximately 1 in

Toughness	300. Bearings under load deform elastically at the contact point between the rolling element and bearing ring. This is influenced by the bearing type, size, form and load.
Installation & Removal	The single row radial ball bearing is a non-separable bearing. Therefore, shafts and housings should be so designated to enable bearing inspection and replacement when necessary.
Axial Location	Improved axial location is obtained with NR and F type bearings

ABEC Ratings: Unfortunately, bearings can be misrepresented, fraudulently manufactured, or can be counterfeited just like many other things today. Given the cost and time involved in manufacturing bearings, there is a lot of temptation to get a higher price for a lower quality bearing, since a typical user would not probably notice the difference until the bearing failed.

Bearing manufacturers have established standards for the quality and precision of bearings, and there are 3 internationally recognized ratings for specifying manufacturing tolerances' of bearings:

- *Annular Bearing Engineering Committee or Council (ABEC) is a US organization.*

- *The International Standards Organization (ISO) is an international organization.*

- *National Standards Organization (DIN) is a German organization.*

Below is a cross-reference that can be used to classify a bearing across these three standards. If a bearing is not classified as an ABEC rated bearing, it is considered to be non-precision or un-rated, and outside the precision standards.

ABEC Bearing Ratings (from highest to lowest)		
ABEC 1	Normal/ISO	P0/DIN
ABEC 3	Class 6/ISO	P6/DIN
ABEC 5	Class 5/ISO	P5/DIN
ABEC 7	Class 4/ISO	P4/DIN
ABEC 9	Class 2/ISO	P2/DIN

These standards are known as ABEC classes as set by the Annular Bearing Engineers Committee of the American Bearing Manufacturer's Association (ABMA). These standards are also accepted by (ANSI) American National Standards Institute and by international agreement for the standards developed by (ISO) International Organization of Standardization.

The ABEC scale is a system of rating the manufacturing tolerance of precision bearings. The system was developed by the Annular Bearing Engineering Council (ABEC), a division of the American Bearing Manufacturers' Association ABMA). The ABMA was formerly known as the Anti-Friction Bearing Manufacturers' Association. Bearings rated under the ABEC systems are typically called "precision bearings", with a rating or class from 1 to 9. ABEC 1 meets a looser tolerance and ABEC 9 meets high precision tight bearing tolerances.

26 | Bushings and Ball Bearings

ABEC Tolerances

All tolerances are in .0001 inches	abec 1	abec 3p	abec 5p	abec 7p	abec 9p
INNER RING (Bore Diameter < 0.7087 inches)					
Bore Tolerance	+0/-3	+0/-2	+0/-2	+0/-2	+0/-2
Radial Runout (Bore 0 0.3937")	3	2	1.5	1	0.5
Radial Runout (Bore 0.3937 - 0.7087")	4	3	1.5	1	0.5
Width Tolerance	+0/-50	+0/-50	+0/-10	+0/-10	+0/-10
Width Variation	-	-	2	1	0.5
Reference Runout with Bore (max)	-	-	3	1	0.5
Groove Runout with Reference Side (max)	-	-	3	1	0.5
Bore 2 Point Out of Round (max)	-	-	1	1	0.5
Bore Taper (max)	-	-	1	1	0.5
OUTER RING (OUTER Diameter < 0.875 inches)					
Outer Diameter Tolerance	+0/-3	+0/-3	+0/-2	+0/-2	+0/-1
Radial Runout (max)	6	4	2	1.5	0.5*
Width Tolerance	+0/-50	+0/-50	+0/-10	+0/-10	+0/-10
Width Variation	-	-	2	1	0.5
Flange Width Tolerance Limits	-	+0/-20	+0/-20	+0/-20	-
Flange Diameter Tolerance Limits	-	+50/-20	+0/-10	+0/-10	-
Groove Runout with Reference Side (max)	-	-	3	2	0.5*
Outside Cylindrical Surface Runout with Reference Side (max)	-	-	3	1.5	0.5

Ceramic Bearings

Ceramic is the new Holy Grail! It's lighter, smoother, stiffer, harder, corrosion resistant, and electrically resistant. These fundamental characteristics allow for a wide range of performance enhancements in bearings. Ceramic bearings dissipate heat quickly, reducing friction and wear while maintaining a precision smooth surface. Today's leading edge ceramics are made with Silicon Nitride (Si3N4) and have characteristics similar to the heat absorbing, highly resilient tiles on the Space Shuttle.

Hybrid Ceramic Bearings

Conventional all steel bearings limit design potential as technology requirements roll forward at a fantastic rate. Ceramic Hybrid bearings using Silicon Nitride balls (Si3N4) meet and exceed today's high tech requirements, offering a long list of characteristics far superior to that of conventional all-steel bearings.

Miniature Bearings For Industry, Hobby & Recreation
Phone: (800) 332-3256 | Email: info@bocabearings.com

Search for replacement fishing reel bearings directly at:
http://www.bocabearings.com/main1.aspx?p=quicksearchkit&cat=5

BOCA BEARING COMPANY
755 NW 17th Ave. #107
Delray Beach, FL 33445 U.S.A.
Toll free phone: (800) 332-3256

Boca Bearing's much anticipated line of ceramic Orange Seal fishing reel bearings have finally arrived. Boca's Orange Seal bearings are the true secret weapon for serious fishing and distance casting. Orange Seal bearings bring cutting edge ceramic technology to the fishing industry with increased casting distance, substantially longer life and overall better performance. Ceramic hybrids are a combination of stainless steel races with ceramic balls. Ceramic balls are virtually frictionless, 1/3 lighter and several times harder than steel, as a result spool startup is faster and sustained spool speeds are much higher. The reduced friction allows some reels to free spool for up to 60 seconds!

The improvement is in the details. ABEC 7 tolerance make the Orange Seal line the closest precision tolerance that the Boca Bearing Company has to offer. Removable, non-contact rubber seals results in a bearing with less drag that requires less maintenance than a typical shielded bearing. Grade 5 ceramic $Si3N4$ balls make the bearing lighter and spin 50% faster than a traditional steel bearing.

Boca Bearing also offers standard Econo Power bearings and Lightning Series ABEC 5 ceramic hybrid bearings. The Econo Power Fishing Reel Bearing kits are the most affordable way to replace stock fishing reel bearings. These ABEC 5 bearings have stainless steel races, balls, retainers and shields. Ceramic Lightning Fishing Reel Bearing kits are intended as an upgrade replacement to stock fishing reel bearings. These ABEC 5 bearings have ceramic balls with stainless steel races, retainers and shields.

To complement and care for fishing reel bearings, the Boca Bearing Company has developed a full line of lubricants known as Lightning Lube. Reel Power Lube is recommended for all moving metal parts and forms a molecular bond with any metal surface. Reel Power fills in the pits and gaps in the metal surface while also providing a thin film coating to improve performance and reduce corrosion. Reel Grease Power Lube is lithium based grease that improves performance, reduces heat, extends life and resists corrosion. Also available are Clean Touch, a bearing cleaner, Bearing Soak for bearing preparation before installation and a super lightweight High Speed Oil, with a viscosity of 1875/9CS.

Drag Systems and Washer Sets

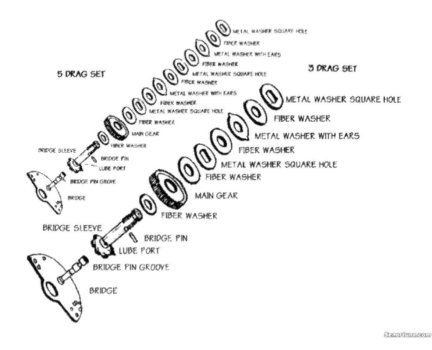

© Photo courtesy of SmoothDrag

What is a drag system?

It's a sort of a clutch which is supposed to let the line unwind in a controlled manner off the reel when a fish pulls so hard that the line is in danger of breaking. There are many different drag arrangements on different kinds or brands of reels. They are all adjustable so you can control the amount of pull it takes to make the line peel off the spool but there is a wide variation from one reel to the next in how precise the adjustment can be and in how smoothly the line slips out. A drag which feeds line out smoothly is very valuable. When a fish suddenly strikes or when an already hooked fish makes a sudden run you want the drag to immediately feed line with no jerks or catches. A sticky drag can cause a line to break in a hurry. The drag should feed line out so that the line never breaks.

There are several different drag set ups. Most involve a series of fiber and metal washers which spin against each other when the drag slips.

In early Mitchells from France, early Ocean City's, early Penn's and others, leather was used as a drag material. As you would expect performance was poor at best. Over the years, other materials were used including carbon, felt, particleboard, and others, these all became sticky over time. Coarse woven carbon fiber (HT-100) soon became the choice for Penn reels; the downside was this material would become sticky if wet or corroded. Shimano found that by adding pure Teflon grease to the coarse woven carbon fiber drag that is "never" failed. This combination found its way into Penn, Okuma, and Daiwa reels. Accurate started out using dry carbon fiber in 1996, and then in 2007 they started adding Cal's Grease and have also had a zero failure rate.

Daiwa uses greased carbon in their Saltist 20 and 30 models, Okuma uses what is called a carbonite drag washer which is greased carbon fiber, Progear used it previously in their Albacore Special and Classic Series but are now out of business.

If your reel has a dry carbon fiber drag system, and you are experiencing stickiness, then simply adding some "Super Slick" grease could be your solution.

Notice in any drag systems, metal washers never touch, it is always metal, fiber, metal, fiber, etc.

When we are talking about 3 Drag Set, 5 Drag Set, etc. the number is determined by counting the number of fiber washers.

Michael Garrison – 13.2 LB Largemouth Bass (May 2009, Birmingham, ALA)

"I use both Carbontex washers and Super Slick in all my drag systems, without a smooth drag I never would have landed this baby!" – **Michael Garrison**

Fishing Reel Care and Maintenance

Following the recommended proper maintenance for your reels will not only increase the lifetime of your reels but also the day to day performance. Typically you should be performing routine maintenance on your reels at least every 3 months, more often if your reels are used excessively.

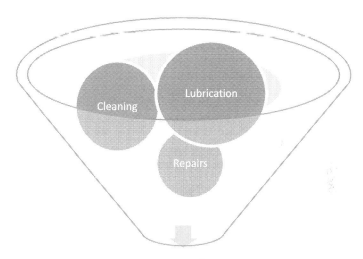

Maximum Performance

Modern reels are complex pieces of equipment; super smooth, multiple bearings, high-tech lightweight materials, you name it. Unfortunately this high-tech gear comes at a price.

Even though most tackle is made from high quality materials like carbon, aviation grade aluminum, stainless steel and even titanium, we practice our sport in a very hostile environment: humidity, UV exposure, extreme temperatures, salt spray, mud, sand, coral....

In spite of the quality of design and material, fishing reels take a beating every time we go out. Does this mean that you should only buy less expensive equipment? Certainly not, however there are some things that you can do to properly care for and maintain your reels, and this book is going to show you how to do that. Saltwater reels should be rinsed with warm freshwater to remove any saltwater residue, dried, and then lubricated appropriately according to the manufacturer. Saltwater corrodes metal parts quickly; a saltwater reel left unmaintained will quickly corrode and cease to function at all.

Tips for protecting reels:

1. Always avoid dipping your reel in water especially saltwater.

2. Avoid hitting your reel against rocks, docks, boat decks, etc. Scratches and dents can expose bare metal and cause corrosion.

3. Never drop a reel in the sand, sand grains can damage drag disks and ball bearings. If you do, stop using it immediately until you service it!

4. Make sure reels are not exposed to saltwater spray on a moving boat. This is where reel covers should always be used.

5. Immediately after each fishing trip, rinse the reel under LOW pressure freshwater, then remove the spool, shake out any excess water and allow to dry before reassembly. Reels should never be soaked for extended periods of time because water will penetrate ball bearings and cause them to rust, even though a ball bearing case might be stainless steel, the bearing itself may not be. Soaking can also distort cork drag plates and cause jerky drags.

6. Always loosen the drag completely whenever the reel is not in use. This will prevent damage to the drag washers due to compression.

7. When storing saltwater reels you should remove all line and backing because the line will hold saltwater residue and can cause corrosion.

8. It is better to not store a reel in a pouch or cover, especially if the reel is wet. It is always better to store the reel on a shelf or inside a cabinet.

9. **Fresh water fishing,** if you fish only a few times per year, have your reel serviced at least once every year, two on the outside. If you fish regularly, have your reel serviced once per year minimum.

10. **For salt water fishing,** if you fish only a few times per year, have your reel serviced a minimum of once per year. If you fish on a regular basis your reel should be serviced two to four times per year. You can determine how often by having it serviced at a two to four month interval then ask the servicer how often he recommends by what it looks like internally. This way you could add or reduce service intervals accordingly while getting the maximum life out of your equipment.

11. **For seasonal fishing** it would be wise to have your reel serviced at the end of the fishing season rather than at the beginning of the next season. If moisture were to get inside your reel, then you put it aside for four or five months, some reel parts may become damaged from corrosion. If you're going to have it serviced anyway, the best time is at the end of the fishing season.

Basic Cleaning Tips

1. Gather the proper cleaning supplies.

    1. We recommend you use Simple Green for a general purpose cleaning compound, Lighter Fluid for bearings, ReelSchematic Chile Pepper Sauce Reel Oil, and ReelSchematic Muscle Grease.

2. Never put metal to metal when working on your reel, all parts are designed to be metal to fiber.

3. Never use gasoline or other petroleum based products to remove dirt and grease from reel parts, it can and will melt plastic parts. Instead use a cleaning product such as Simple Green which will not hurt plastic and fiber parts.

4. When you are greasing gears, always apply the grease to the bottoms of the teeth, this will avoid grease splatter. Remember a light coat is all you need so don't apply to much.

5. Clean bearings with lighter fluid to remove dirt and buildup. After you've got them all clean make sure they spin, if they don't then you know they are not clean enough yet. When you get them cleaned oil them with ReelSchematic Chile Pepper Sauce Oil, you should only need one drop for each bearing.

Basic Tools

Screwdrivers

1/8" Standard
3/16" Standard
5/16" Standard
No.0 Phillips
No.1 Phillips
No.2 Phillips

Wrenches

Socket Wrenches

5mm or 3/16"
6mm or 1/14"
7mm or 9/32"
8 mm or 5/16"
9mm or 11/32"
10mm or 13/32"
12mm or 15/32"
14mm or 9/16"

Pliers

Long needle nose
Diagonal Cutting
Snap Ring Pliers

Others

Standard Sewing Needle
Toothpicks
Cotton Swabs
Lint Free Cloths
Tweezers
6" Calipers
Specialty Shimano and Penn

Recommended Lubricants

ReelSchematic Chile Pepper Sauce
ReelSchematic Muscle Grease
ReelSchematic Muscle Lube
ReelSchematic Super Slick

Accurate Boss Reels require a 3/8" combo wrench and a #7 torx bit, you will need to grind down the torx bit to give it a long shank as the screw holes are deep on accurate reels. Some older models have a hex head instead of torx.

Lubrication

The main purpose of any lubricant in a reel is to reduce wear. Generally grease will be used on bushings, gear teeth, and shafts to prevent metal to metal contact. The most essential property of grease is its viscosity, you'll hear this term a lot when referring to both grease and oil. **Viscosity** is a measure of the resistance of a fluid which is being deformed by either shear stress or extensional stress. In everyday terms (and for fluids only), viscosity is "thickness". Thus, water is "thin", having a lower viscosity, while honey is "thick" having a higher viscosity. The viscosity of the grease you are using must be sufficient to resist extrusion from the contacting metal surfaces by the pressure generated by heavy loads, and it must be unaffected by temperature and water.

The latest in nano-technological advances is Tungsten Disulfide (WS_2). The most lubricious material known to modern science is now being combined with high quality synthetic lubricants to produce a grease that is unmatched by others. Tungsten Disulfide can be used in high temperatures and high pressure application. It offers temperature resistance from -4° F to 1472° F, and a load bearing weight of 300,000 psi.

"Super Slick" is specifically formulated with

Tungsten Disulfide to provide the best grease known to science for fishing reels.

Tungsten Disulfide (WS2) is one of the most lubricious materials known to science. With Coefficient of Friction at 0.03, it offers excellent dry lubricity unmatched to any other substance. It can also be used in high temperature and high pressure applications. It offers temperature resistance from -450° F (-270° C) to 1200° F (650° C) in normal atmosphere and from -305° F (-188° C) to 2400° F (1316° C) in Vacuum. Load bearing property of coated film is extremely high at 300,000 psi.

Tungsten Disulfide (WS2) can be used instead of Molybdenum Disulfide (MoS2) and Graphite in almost all applications, and even more. Molybdenum and Tungsten are from same chemical family. Tungsten is heavier and more stable. Molybdenum Disulfide (Also known as Moly Disulfide) till now has been extremely popular due to cheaper price, easier availability and strong and innovative marketing. Tungsten Disulfide is not new chemical and has been around as long as Moly, and is used extensively by NASA, military, aerospace and automotive industry.

Till few years ago, price was Tungsten Disulfide was almost 10 times that of Molybdenum Disulfide. But since then price of Molybdenum Disulfide has doubled every six months. Now the prices of both chemicals are within comparable range. Now, it makes more economic sense to use superior dry lubricant (Tungsten Disulfide) and improve the quality and competitiveness of final product.

Tungsten Disulfide offers excellent lubrication under extreme conditions of Load, Vacuum and Temperature. The properties below show that Tungsten Disulfide offers excellent thermal stability and oxidation resistance at higher temperatures. WS2 has thermal stability advantage of 93°C (200°F) over MoS2. Coefficient of Friction of WS2 actually reduces at higher loads.

"Super Slick" is a technological breakthrough in nano-lubricants. Super Slick has the lowest coefficient of friction of any grease in the world; it offers lubricity unmatched by any other substance! If you're looking for the absolute best lubricating grease in the world for your reels this is it! **Tungsten Disulfide**, which is known to be the most lubricious material known to science, was once only used extensively by NASA, Aerospace, and Military because of its price. Today it is available to you in our newest "Super Slick" Grease.

- The lowest coefficient of friction of any substance in the world - .015
- Temperature resistance from -4 F (-20 C) to 1472 F (800 C)
- It will hold up in even the worst of weather conditions!
- Excellent extreme pressure properties with loading bearing up to 300,000 psi
- Extremely high resistance to water, rust and humidity
- High dropping point of 608° F which means it does not solidify at high temperatures
- 100x better than any grease you are presently using!

Available at www.reelschematic.com

Typical Bait Casting Reel Lubrication

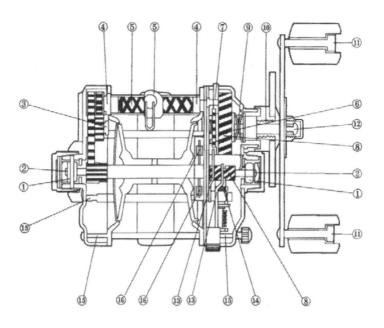

© Photo courtesy of Daiwa Corporation

Fishing Reel Care and Maintenance 101 | 43

#	Part Name	Lubrication	How Often	Key Point Care
1	Ball Bearing	Medium or heavy oil Light or medium grease	After each day of fishing Once every 3 weeks	Do not drop or hit. Always keep bearing greased inside and out
2	Spool Shaft	Medium or heavy oil Light or medium grease	After each day of fishing Once every 3 weeks	Contact or meshing areas of ball bearing or pinion gear
3	Cog wheel & cog wheel holder shaft	Light or medium oil Heavy Oil	Once every 3 weeks Once every 2 months	Do not use heavy grease
4	Worm shaft on shield bushing left & right side	Light or medium oil	After each day of fishing	—
5	Worm shaft & line guide pin	Medium or heavy oil Light or medium grease	Once every 3 weeks Once every 2 months	Regularly inspect for dirt, grit, and salt – keep clean
6	Spool drag washer	Medium or heavy grease	Once every 3 months	Contains special Teflon or graphite grease for better performance
7	A/R claw and gear shaft click	Medium or heavy grease sparingly all areas.	Once every 3 months	Do not disturb the claw spring arrangement
8	Drive gear & pinion gear	Medium or heavy grease	Once every 3 months	Make sure all surfaces are lubricated in appropriate amounts
9	Drag spring & gear shaft assembly	Medium or heavy grease	Once every 3 months	Make sure all surfaces are lubricated

Lubrication

10	Star drag	Medium or heavy grease	Once every 3 months	After each day of fishing, loosen drag adjustment to preserve the spring and washer life
11	Handle knob or shaft	Light or medium heavy oil Light or medium grease	After each day fishing Once every 3 weeks	Inspect regularly. Do not allow lube to dry to eliminate wear
12	Set plate on gear shaft	Medium or heavy oil	Once every 3 weeks	Be certain to remove nut plate screw & plate. Take off nut & screw
13	Clutch lever & set plate post	Medium or heavy grease	Once every 3 months	Lubricate in appropriate amounts
14	Set plate spring A B Pinion yoke spring	Medium or heavy oil	Once every 3 months	Lubricate in appropriate amounts
15	Frame assembly post	Medium or heavy grease	Once every 2 months	Lubricate in appropriate amounts
16	Spool brake collar shaft	Do Not Lubricate	Once every 3 months	No lubrication
17	Spool line	Do Not Lubricate		If saltwater fishing, spool should be removed after each trip and rinsed with freshwater

Typical Spinning Reel Lubrication

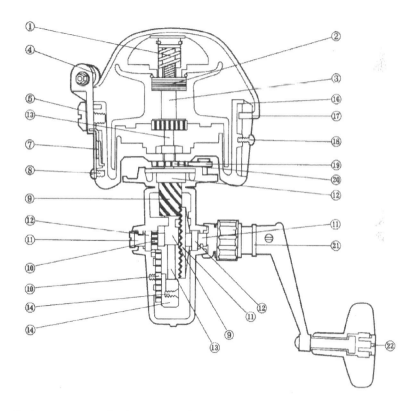

© Photo courtesy of Daiwa Corporation

Lubrication

#	Part Name	Lubrication	How Often	Key Point Care
1	Drag Knob	Medium or heavy grease	Once every 3 weeks	Do not over lubricate, and do not change the sequence of washers
2	Spool Washer	Medium or heavy grease	Once every 3 weeks	Contains special Teflon or graphite grease for better performance
3	Main shaft	Light or medium heavy grease	After each fishing day	Make certain the spool washer is present
4	Line Roller	Light or heavy oil Light or medium grease	After each day fishing Once every 3 weeks	Lubricate in appropriate amounts
5	Arm Lever & Screw	Medium or heavy oil Light or medium heavy grease	After each day fishing Once every 4 weeks	Lubricate in appropriate amounts
6	Arm Lever Screw	Medium or heavy grease	Once every 3 months	Lubricate in appropriate amounts
7	Bail Spring	Medium or heavy grease	Once every 3 months	
8	Bail Spring Cover Screw	Medium or heavy grease	Once every 3 months	
9	Pinion Gear	Light or medium grease	Once every 3 months	Lubricate all surfaces with an appropriate amount

Fishing Reel Care and Maintenance 101 | 47

#	Part Name	Lubrication	How Often	Key Point Care
10	Osc. Gear, Osc. Pinion	Medium grease	Once every 3 months	Lubricate all surfaces with an appropriate amount
11	Drive Gear	Medium or heavy grease	Once every 3 months	Gear teeth & shaft. Lubricate with appropriate amounts
12	Ball Bearing	Heavy Oil or light grease / Medium or heavy grease	Once every 3 months	Freshwater reel only Saltwater reel, all surfaces
13	Main Shaft	Medium or heavy oil / Light or medium grease	Once every 3 months 1. 2.	Freshwater Saltwater all surfaces
14	Oscillating Slider	Medium grease	Once every 3 months	Lubricate in appropriate amounts
15	Osc. Slider Screw	Medium grease	Once every 3 months	
16	Rotor assembly	Medium or heavy grease	Once every 3 months	Left & Right Side
17	Ball Assembly	Medium or heavy oil / Medium or heavy grease	After each day fishing Once every 3 weeks	

Lubrication

18	Bail Holder Screw	Medium grease	Once every 3 months	
19	A/R Claw & Screw	Heavy Oil Medium or light grease	Once every 3 months	Do not alter claw spring arrangement
20	Ratchet & Screw	Light or medium grease	Once every 3 months	
21	Handle Washer & Screw	Medium oil or grease	Once every 3 weeks	
22	Handle Knob & Shaft	1. Medium or heavy oil 2. Light or medium heavy grease	1. After each day fishing 2. Once every 3 weeks	

Shimano Trinidad\Torium Drag Upgrade

This tutorial is provided to assist those of you who may be interested in performing upgrade of the

drag system of your Shimano Trinidad 16, 16N, 20 and 30, and Torium 16, 20 and 30. These upgrades are designed to

enhance the performance of your Shimano Trinidad or Torium reel by increasing the drag range in the above listed reels manufactured prior to 2005.

Parts included in Drag Upgrade Kit:
1. Upgraded side plate
2. Upgraded Drive Shaft
3. Upgraded Drag Plate (key washer)

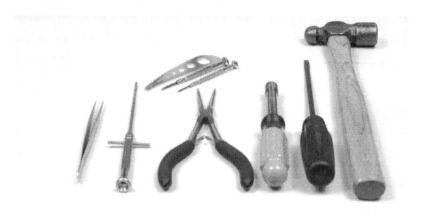

Tools need for the upgrade:
1. 10mm nut driver
2. Small Philips screwdriver
3. Medium Philips screwdriver
4. Small flat screwdriver
5. Medium flat screwdriver
6. Shimano Wrench (TGT0355)
7. Needle nose pliers
8. Rubber Mallet

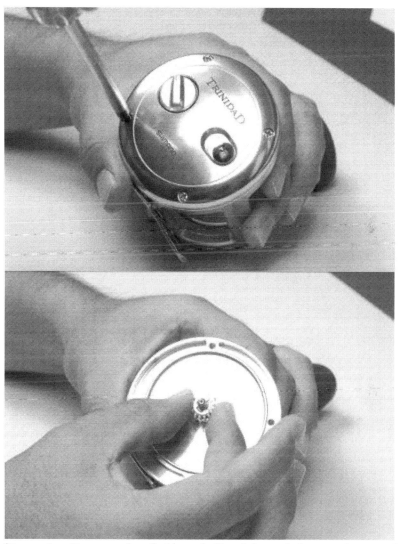

Step 1: Removal of the left side plate and spool assembly

Remove spool assembly by removing the four left side plate screws with a medium Philips screwdriver or flathead screwdriver.

Step 2: Removal of handle assembly
Remove handle nut plate screw and handle nut using a small Philips screwdriver. Remove handle assembly by using the Shimano Wrench.

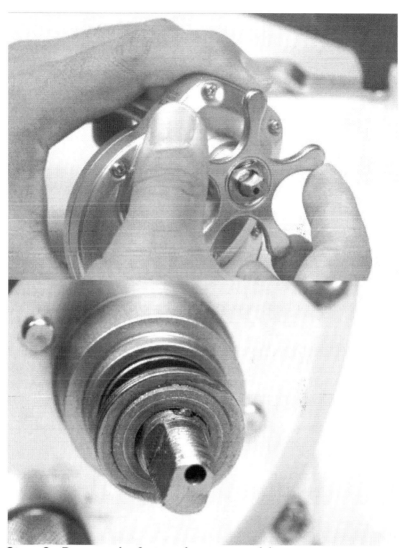

Step 3: Removal of star drag assembly
Back off star drag (caution: click pin TGT0295 may pop out!) and remove all washers and bearing seal located under star drag.

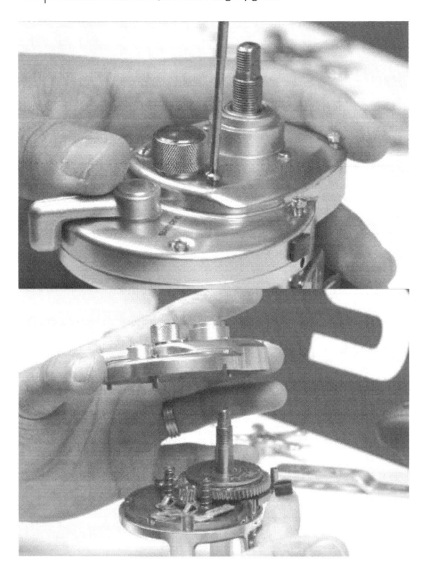

Step 4: Removal of right side plate
Remove all right side plate screws (8 total). Side plate and line clip can be removed now.

Fishing Reel Care and Maintenance 101 | 55

Step 5: Removal of drive gears

Remove the roller clutch inner tube, drive gear assembly, drag washer (A) (located under drive gear), yoke springs (2 total), pinion gear, yoke, yoke plate.

Step 6: Removal of anti-reverse assembly
Remove anti-reverse pawl keeper screws (2 total) and anti-reverse pawl keeper. Remove anti-reverse pawl and anti-reverse ratchet.

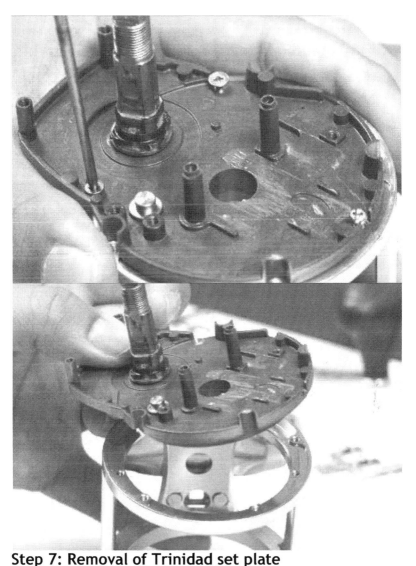

Step 7: Removal of Trinidad set plate
On Trinidad reels, remove set plate screws (3 total). Thereafter, remove set plate from one-piece frame. Torium reels do not a removable set plate. Please skip this step if you are working on a Torium reel.

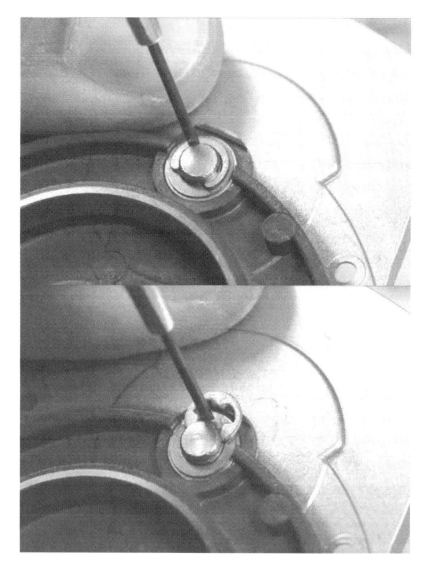

Step 8: Removal of drive shaft retainer clip for Trinidad reels

Using a small flathead screwdriver, carefully remove the drive shaft retainer clip. Remove drive shaft.

Step 8: Removal of drive shaft retainer clip for Torium reels

The drive shaft retainer clip is located on the frame and is exposed when the spool assembly is removed.

60 | Shimano Trinidad\Torium Drag Upgrade

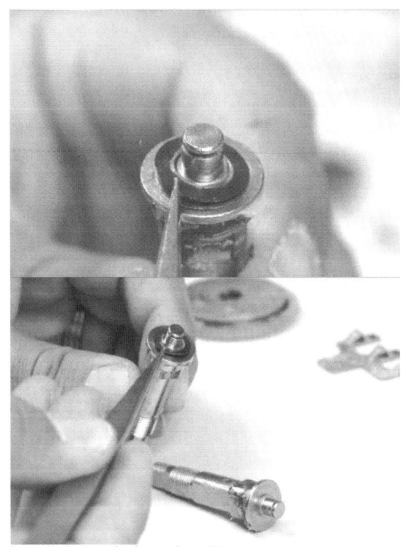

Step 9: Drive shaft washer (B)
Remove drive shaft washer (B). Transfer washer (B) onto new upgraded drive shaft. Also, remove the click spring from original drive shaft and transfer to upgraded drive shaft. (TGT0296)

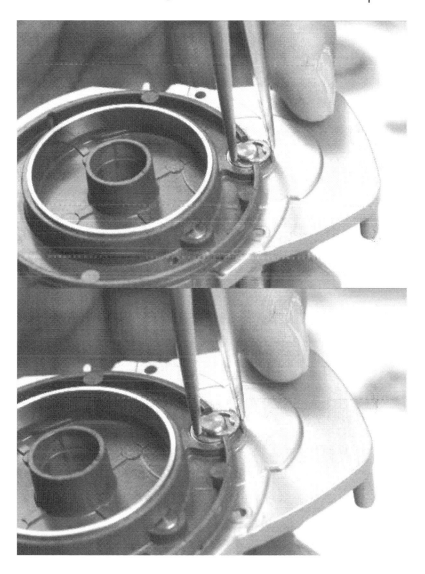

Step 10: Installation of upgraded drive shaft on Trinidad reels

Install new drive shaft and install drive shaft retainer clip by using needle nose pliers.

Step 10: Installation of upgraded drive shaft on Torium reels.
Use needle nose pliers to install drive shaft retainer clip.

Step 11: Re-installation of anti-reverse assembly

Re-install anti-reverse pawl and anti-reverse ratchet. Be cautious not to damage the anti-reverse pawl. Re-install anti-reverse pawl keeper and anti-reverse pawl keeper screws with a small Phillips or flathead screwdriver.

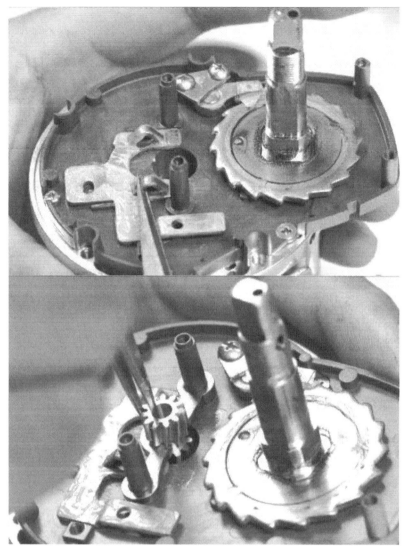

Step 12: Reinstallation of yoke plate, yoke and pinion gear

Re-install yoke plate, pinion gear and yoke, and yoke springs (2 total). Note: the yoke has bevels on one side. Make sure that the bevels face down towards the yoke plate.

Step 13: Re-installation of main drive gear and upgraded drag plate (key washer)

Re-install drag washer (A) (located under the drive gear assembly. Re-install drive gear assembly with new drag plate (key washer). Ensure that the key washer is positioned with the flat side down as pictured above on right.

Step 14: Re-installation of roller clutch inner tube
Re-install roller clutch inner tube. Make sure that the tongues on the inner tube engage the grooves on the drag plate (key washer).

Fishing Reel Care and Maintenance 101 | 67

Step 15: Removal of side plate bearing
Remove side plate bearing from original side plate.

Step 16: Removal of roller clutch bearing
Remove roller clutch bearing from original side plate using 10MM nut driver and rubber mallet or hammer.

Fishing Reel Care and Maintenance 101 | 69

Step 17: Installation of roller clutch bearing into upgraded side plate
Install roller clutch bearing into new upgraded side plate by using 10MM nut driver and rubber mallet or hammer. Make sure that the roller clutch bearing sits flush with the inside edge of side plate.

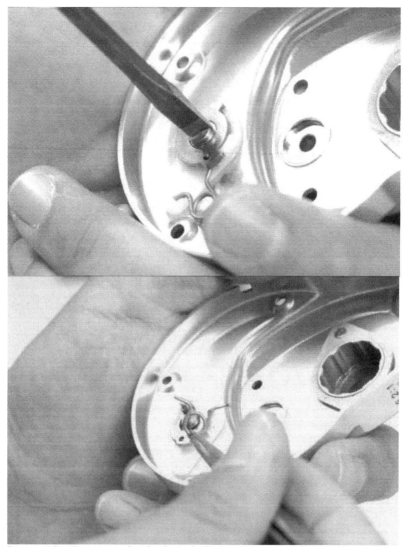

Step 18: Removal of clutch lever assembly
Use a medium flathead screwdriver to remove clutch lever screw, eccentric cam, clutch spring, eccentric cam bushing, smoother (nylon washer) and clutch lever from original side plate.

Fishing Reel Care and Maintenance 101 | 71

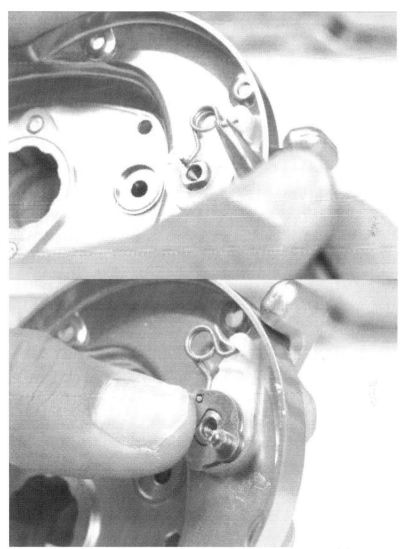

Step 19: Installation of clutch lever assembly onto upgraded side plate
Install smoother (nylon washer), clutch lever, eccentric cam bushing, clutch spring, clutch cam and clutch lever screw onto new upgraded side plate.

Step 20: Cast control cap and "o" ring
Remove cast control cap from original side plate. Use a small flathead screwdriver to remove "O" ring from original sideplate. Install "O" ring and cast control cap onto new upgraded sideplate.

Step 21: Installation of new side plate and line clip
Install side plate and line clip onto reel with the 8 side plate screws. Make sure that the clutch cam and yoke plate engage one another, otherwise, the clutch will not work.

Step 22: Side plate bearing, bearing seal and thrust washer
Install side plate bearing, bearing seal, and bearing thrust washer in this order.

Fishing Reel Care and Maintenance 101 | 75

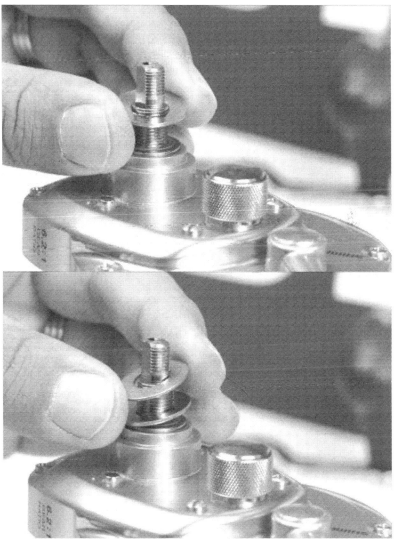

Step 23: Re-installation of drag spring washers
Re-install drag spring washer (heavy) and drag spring washer (light). Springs should face each other like this: ()

76 | Shimano Trinidad\Torium Drag Upgrade

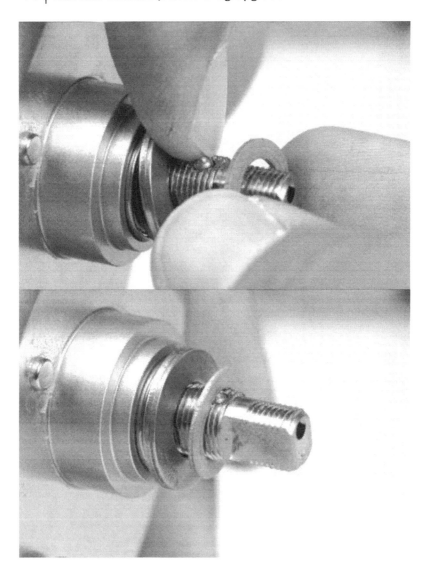

Step 24: Re-installation of click spring
Re-install click pin by using the star drag washer (TGT0266) to hold it in place.

Fishing Reel Care and Maintenance 101 | 77

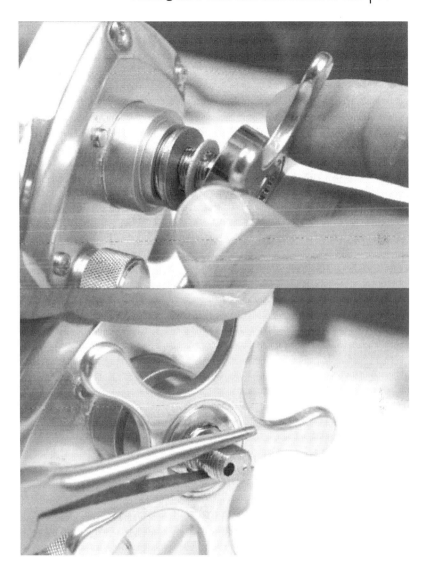

Step 25: Re-installation of star drag
Re-install star drag by turning it clockwise until click pin engages the star drag.

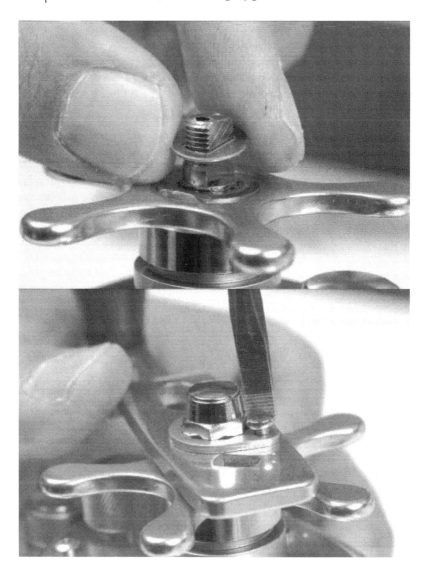

Step 26: Re-installation of handle assembly
Re-install handle shaft shield, handle assembly, handle nut using the Shimano Wrench. Re-install handle nut plate and handle nut plate screw.

Fishing Reel Care and Maintenance 101 | 79

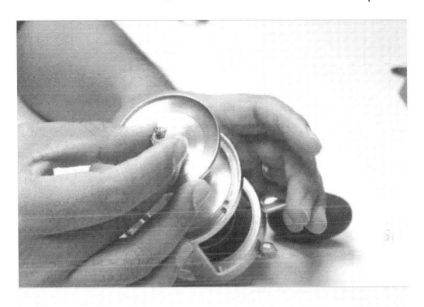

Step 27: Re-installation of spool and left side plate
Insert spool assembly into reel. Re-install left side plate and side plate screws (4 total) with a medium Phillips or flathead screwdriver. Congratulations! Your drag upgrade is now complete!

Daiwa Saltist 30H
Dr. Antony Wright (sealine.co.za)

Before you start, tape up your line with masking tape to prevent getting oil and grease on it.

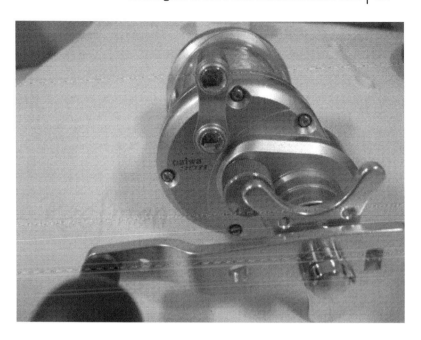

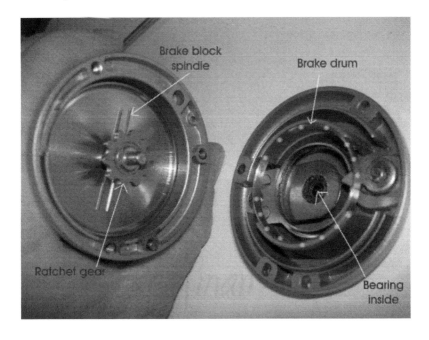

Fishing Reel Care and Maintenance 101 | 83

Fishing Reel Care and Maintenance 101 | 85

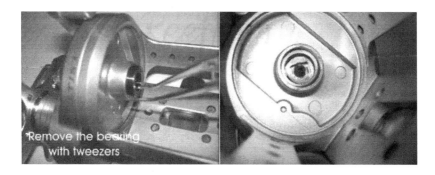

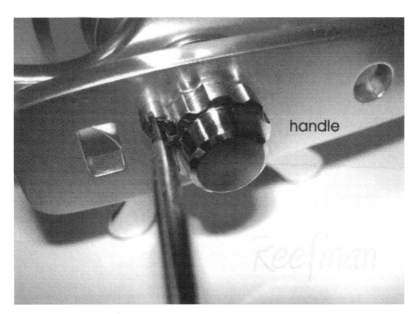

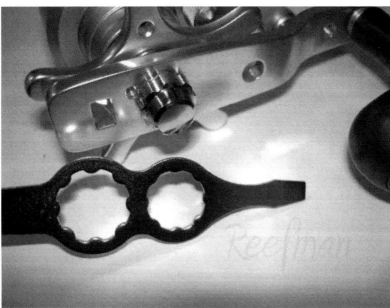

Fishing Reel Care and Maintenance 101

Fishing Reel Care and Maintenance 101 | 89

Daiwa Saltist 30H (40 & 50)

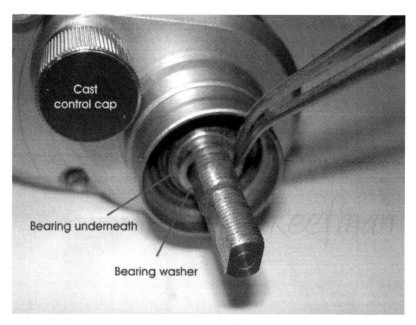

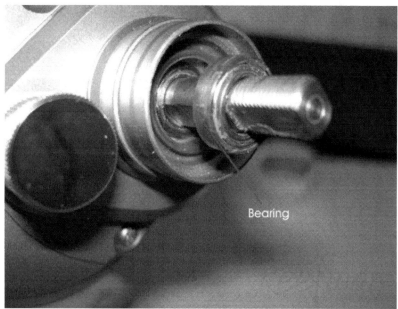

Fishing Reel Care and Maintenance 101 | 91

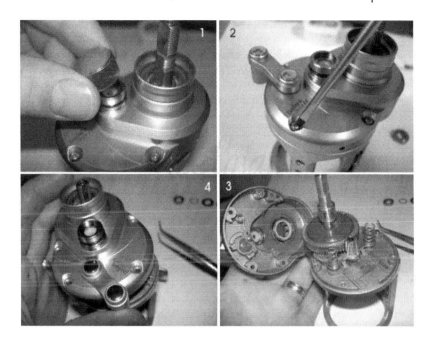

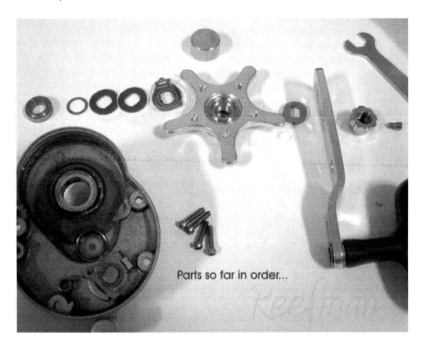

Parts so far in order...

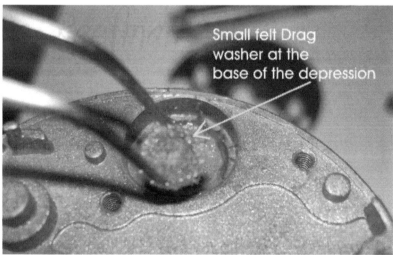

Small felt Drag washer at the base of the depression

Fishing Reel Care and Maintenance 101

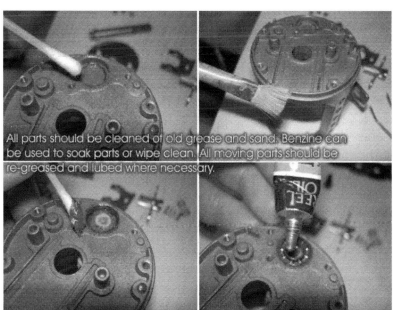

All parts should be cleaned of old grease and sand. Benzine can be used to soak parts or wipe clean. All moving parts should be re-greased and lubed where necessary.

Re-grease moving parts carefully with a quality grease.
A light wiping of all parts with Q20 will help repel water.

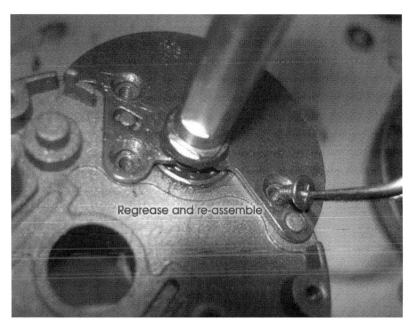

Regrease and re-assemble

Lightly grease the working parts, and re-assemble.

Drag washers are best either left ungreased or greased very lightly with a TEFLON based Grease.

Fishing Reel Care and Maintenance 101 | 103

Fishing Reel Care and Maintenance 101

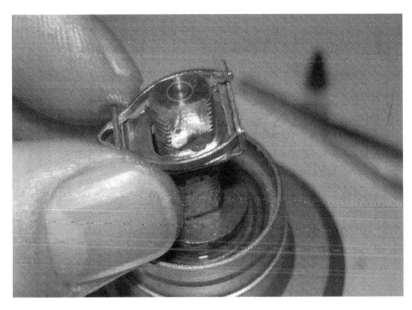

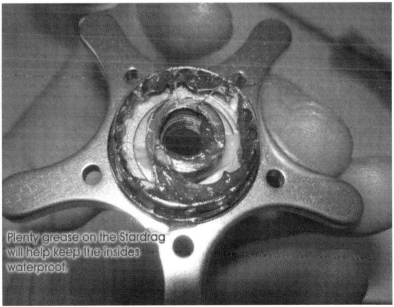

Plenty grease on the Stardrag will help keep the insides waterproof.

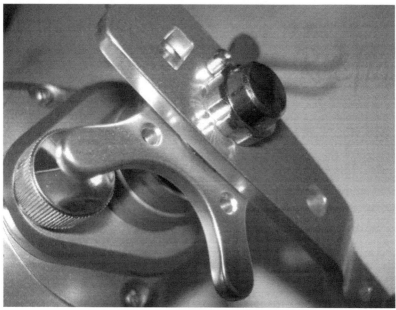

Fishing Reel Care and Maintenance 101 | 109

Don't forget to oil the bearing inside the Brake drum.

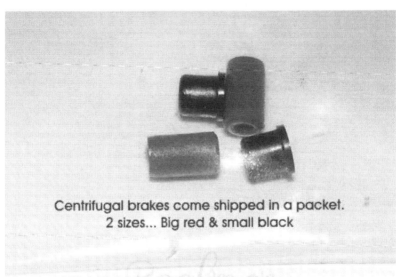

Centrifugal brakes come shipped in a packet.
2 sizes... Big red & small black

Place them on the brake spindles.

Don't forget the Driveshaft bearing.

Fishing Reel Care and Maintenance 101 | 111

When replacing the spool make sure the Cast control knob is very loose, or the spool won't fit back in & the side plate won't close!

Completed, average time is 30-40 minutes

Penn 500, 501, Jigmaster
Dr. Antony Wright (sealine.co.za)

Maintenance guide for disassembly, cleaning, lubrication and reassembly.

Fishing Reel Care and Maintenance 101 | 113

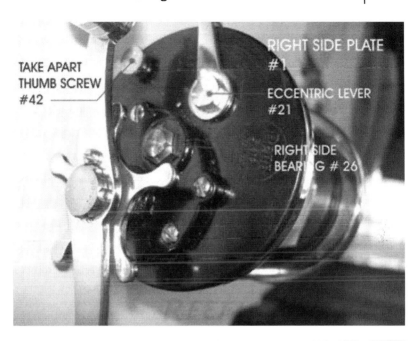

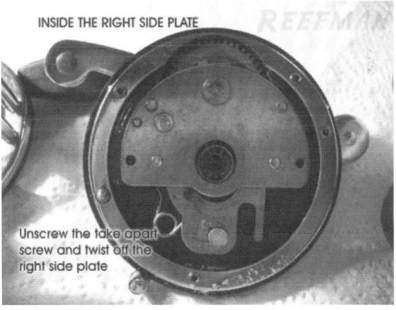

RIGHT INNER SIDE RING #2

Inspect for sand, the Reel killer!

Fishing Reel Care and Maintenance 101 | 115

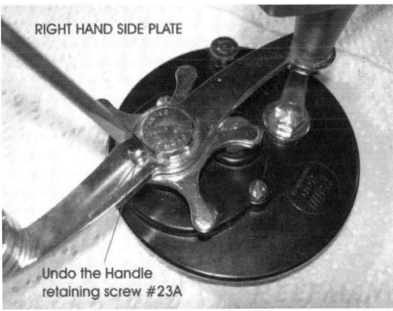

Undo the handle screw #23

Remove the Handle #24

Fishing Reel Care and Maintenance 101 | 117

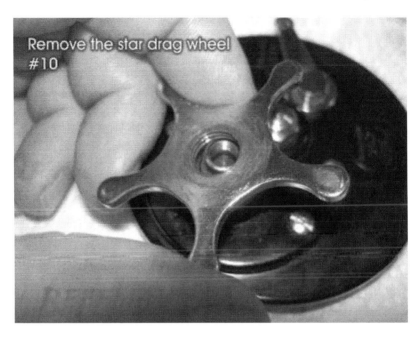

Remove the star drag wheel #10

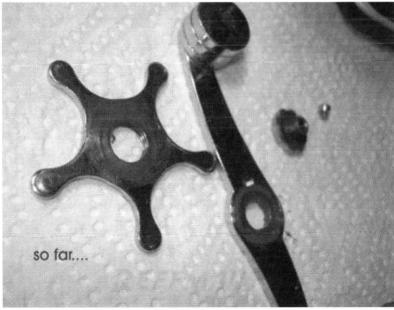

so far....

Undo the Right side bearing #26

Fishing Reel Care and Maintenance 101

Undo the Lower bridge screws #16

Bridge #3

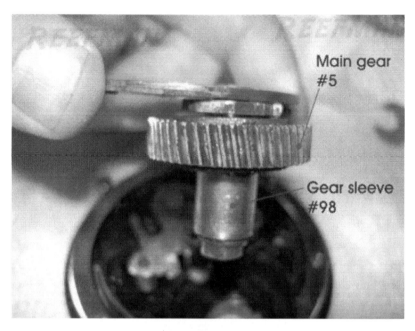

Underneath the bridge gear...

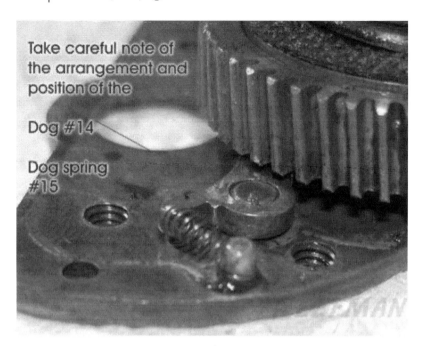

Take careful note of the arrangement and position of the

Dog #14

Dog spring #15

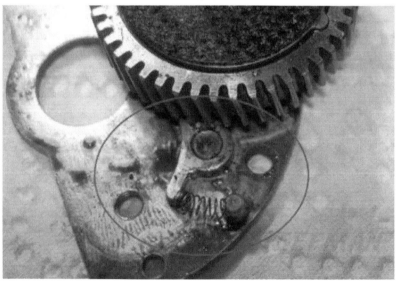

Fishing Reel Care and Maintenance 101 | 123

Remove the gear sleeve

Tension spring #8

Drag washers

Remove the drag washers
#7

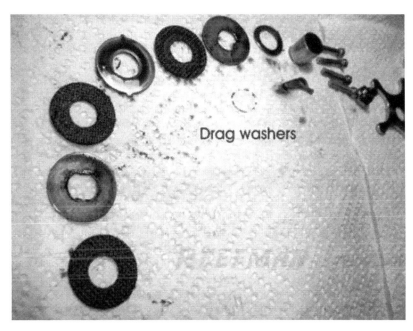

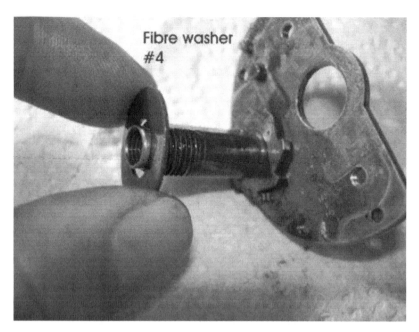

So far....

Unhook the Eccentric Jack

The Pinion Yoke #12

Remove the Yoke springs

Notice the pieces of Mono that have slipped in between the spool and body

Fishing Reel Care and Maintenance 101 | 131

Fishing Reel Care and Maintenance 101

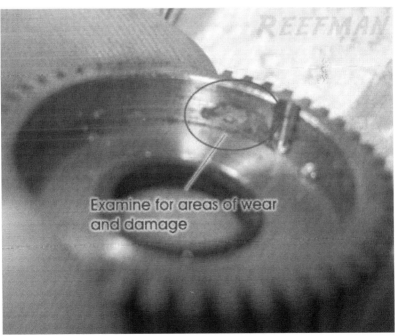

Now we start on the Inner ring framework by undoing the screws of the Spacer bars #37

Fishing Reel Care and Maintenance 101

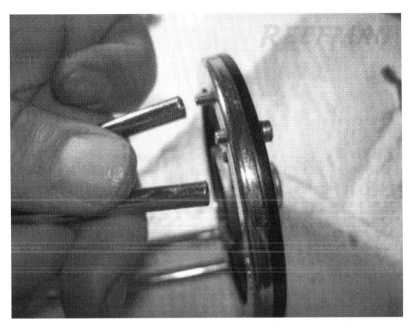

Left side bearing and spring #40 and #41 commonly known as the Cast Control Knob

Click spring #62

Click tongue #35

Inspect for wear and tear - notice the chunk thats been taken out of the tongue...

Sand, sand, everywhere...

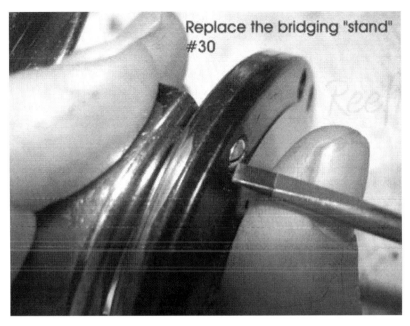

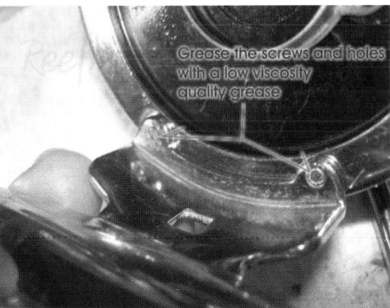

Replace the spacing poles and the outer ring

Fishing Reel Care and Maintenance 101 | 141

Grease up and re-assemble

Lightly grease the drag washers with a Teflon grease

Replace the anti-reverse ratchet and spring after greasing well

Fishing Reel Care and Maintenance 101 | 145

Daiwa Fuego Breakdown

You can breakdown the Daiwa Fuego Reel with just a few basic tools:

Small Standard Screwdriver
Small Needle Nose Pliers or Hemostats
Small Knife or other small bladed device

Figure 1

(Figure 1) Let's start by removing the top cap on the handle, turn the reel on its side and look underneath the handle approximately where the arrows are pointing in the photo above you will see the two clips that holding the cap on, use your small screwdriver to gently pop them up and remove the cap.

Figure 2

(Figure 2) Next use the small needle nose pliers to remove the center nut holding the handle on. (Notice the two slots where the top cap was held on)

During reassembly be careful that you do not strip the threads when putting the nut back on.

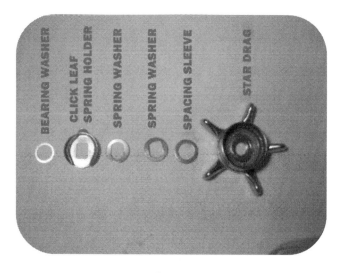

Figure 3

(Figure 3) After you have removed the handle, unscrew the star drag (counter clockwise) to fully remove it, paying attention to the order of the washers underneath as you remove them. You should lay them out in order so that during reassembly you can reverse the order to ensure you put them back correctly.

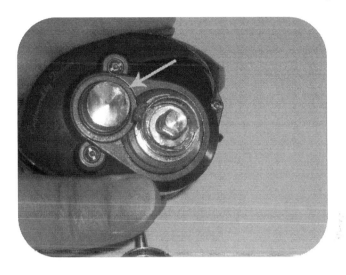

Figure 4

(Figure 4) Next remove the cast control knob by fully unscrewing it (counter clockwise), and removing the pinion shaft as picture in Figure 5.

Figure 5

Figure 6

Check the rubber seal on the cast control for any damage or wear, the seal is very important for keeping water out of the inside of the reel and should be replaced if damaged. You should also use a thin film coating of good quality grease on the seal to keep it pliable and in good condition.

Fishing Reel Care and Maintenance 101 | 153

Figure 7

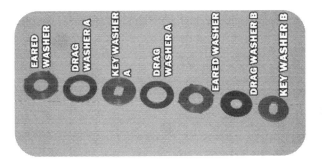

Figure 8

During disassembly of the Drag Washer set, play close attention to the order of the washers. Remember metal never goes against metal; it is always metal/fiber/metal/fiber.

UPGRADE ADVICE:

This is a perfect time to replace the drag washers with Carbontex Fiber Drag Washers from SmoothDrag. Cost is about $8.00. During installation coat them with a liberal amount of Star Drag Grease. (www.smoothdrag.com)

Be very careful when handling the drag washers as they are very fragile and can be broken easily, if one breaks you must replace it with a new one.

After removal of the Drag Washer Configuration this is what you should now see.

Figure 9

Figure 9 shows a picture of the pinion gear and the yoke, notice the slot in the pinion gear that fits right into the yoke. On earlier reels the pinion was made of brass which had to be replaced frequently. (Lew's reels are an example of this early practice)

Figure 10

(Figure 10) To remove the other side plate you must loosen the Set Plate Screw (it does not come all the way out) then using a counterclockwise motion twist the side plate and pull straight out to remove it.

The worm shaft can be disassembled by removing the worm shaft retaining clip. The guide shaft can be disassembled by unscrewing the stabilizer bar.

Fishing Reel Care and Maintenance 101 | 157

Figure 11

Remove the spool by sliding it carefully out the side plate, inspect the spool bearing for any damage and that it spins freely. If it is damaged or does not spin freely it should be replaced, this will cause problems with casting distance and overall performance of the reel.

Fishing Line

Line is arguably the single most important equipment item for any angler. We discuss line here because it is essential to the proper operation of any reel and different types of line and line weights will affect how your reel reacts.

Types of Fishing Line

Monofilament

In 1938, DuPont announced the discovery of nylon, a "group of new synthetic superpolymers" that could be made into textile fibers stronger and more elastic than cotton, silk, wool, or rayon. The next year, DuPont began commercial production of nylon monofilament fishing line. This new line, primitive by today's standards, didn't catch on immediately; older fishing lines, particularly braided Dacron, remained popular for the next two decades. In 1958, however, DuPont introduced Stren, a thinner line of more uniform quality that could be used with different types of reels, including newly introduced spinning and spincasting tackle. This line was quickly embraced by fishermen, and led to a boom in sportfishing popularity because it helped make fishing much easier.

Monofilament products remain popular, accounting for more than two-thirds of all fishing lines sold. As the name suggests, this is a single-component product. It is formed through an extrusion process in which molten plastic is formed into a strand through a die. This process is relatively inexpensive, producing a less costly product--that being the main reason mono is so widely popular.

But it's important to remember that cheaper brands of monofilament usually don't receive the quality-control attention, additives and attention in the finishing process that premium-grade lines receive. As a result, they may not offer the superb blend of tensile strength, limpness, abrasion resistance, and knot strength characteristic of more expensive monos. In other words, you get what you pay for. Cheap off-brand monos usually don't perform as well as more expensive name brands, so "buyers beware." If you decide to use monofilament, test several name brands and stick with those you come to know and trust.

Braided

Before the discovery of nylon, braided Dacron was the most popular line. Dacron possessed poor knot strength, low abrasion resistance and little stretch, however, so it was used much less after superior nylon monofilaments were introduced. Today, it maintains only a very small niche in the marketplace, being used primarily by some catfishermen, who believe its softness improves their catch rate; as backing material on fly reels; and, for a few anglers, as a big-game trolling product.

In the early 1990s, gel-spun and aramid fibers such as Spectra, Kevlar and Dyneema entered the fishing line market, creating a new category of braided lines often called "superlines" or "microfilaments." These synthetic fibers are thin and incredibly strong (more than 10 times stronger than steel). Individual fiber strands are joined through an intricate, time-consuming braiding process to produce ultrathin, superstrong, sensitive, yet expensive lines.

Anglers who experimented with early superlines were frustrated by low knot strength, backlashes, poor coloration, damaged equipment, impossible snags, and more. To many, these disadvantages outweighed the benefits of strength, microdiameter, and ultra sensitivity -- particularly considering the exorbitant costs. However; makers of superlines have made continual advances and improvements to the raw material fibers and the process that converts them into fishing line. Coloration, castability, and strength have all been improved, overcoming some early disadvantages.

Lures dive deeper and faster when connected to superlines. And because it's smaller in diameter, superline is less visible to fish than monofilament, and anglers can spool more line on their reels. Superlines have little stretch, transmitting strikes instantly to the rod tip, thus providing more positive hook sets. Plus, superlines allow longer casts, making them ideal for shore-bound anglers. High break strength and low stretch permit better manhandling of big fish.

Saltwater anglers use most of the braided superlines. Sometimes, the line is used as a backing for mono, allowing anglers to use small reels while increasing line capacity. Many anglers prefer the softness of braid for vertical jigging and trolling.

Superlines require a palomar knot for best results. Put mono backing on your reel before spooling superlines to prevent "slipping" on the reel and to conserve line. This also adds firmness to the spool for better casting and less backlashes. Tie a Uni knot to connect to the mono.

Do not overfill reels with superline. Overfilling creates loose strands after a cast and more backlashes. Fill to one-eighth inch from the spool rim.

A more recent innovation is fused line, made by fusing, rather than braiding, the gel-spun fibers. This process produces what appears to be a single-strand line that is also ultrathin, superstrong, and very sensitive. These lines are larger in diameter and offer a bit less strength than original braids, but they are somewhat easier to cast and tie, and generally more affordable.

Fluorocarbon

Fluorocarbon is a polymer that's nearly invisible in water because it has an almost identical refractive index (an indication of the degree at which light refracts or bends as it passes through a substance). It is inert, so it resists deterioration by sunlight, gasoline, battery acid, or DEET (a common ingredient in insect repellents). And it doesn't absorb water. Fluorocarbon fishing leaders originated in Japan, where anglers are particularly fussy about bait presentations. Japanese fisheries are heavy pressured, so lifelike bait presentations are important. Nearly invisible fluorocarbon lines enhanced this quality.

Ultimately, U.S. anglers began using fluorocarbon leaders, primarily in saltwater and fly fishing applications, for the same reason the Japanese were using it -- low visibility. It caught on when anglers reported catching more fish with it. The original fluorocarbon leaders were stiff and very expensive, but new technologies have produced more flexible fluorocarbon at more affordable prices.

Fluorocarbon certainly offers advantages in clear-water situations where fish are heavily pressured or slow to bite. Also, because fluorocarbon does not absorb water, it won't weaken or increase in stretch like nylon fishing line. Added density makes fluorocarbon very abrasion-resistant, so it's ideal for rough conditions, and makes it sink faster than nylon lines, so lures dive deeper and faster. And because fluorocarbon stretches slower and less than nylon, particularly when compared to wet nylon, it's much more sensitive.

Fluorocarbon lines, like superlines, require special attention. The Trilene knot is the best to use with this type line. Make all 5 wraps when tying the knot, and excessively wet the line before cinching the knot to prevent line weakening. Always test the knot before fishing.

Fluorocarbons are still stiffer than nylon, even when wet. This requires more attentiveness to the line when casting, and finer "balance" of tackle. If heavier fluorocarbon line is used on lighter rods, reels and lures, anglers will experience more difficulty. Baitcasting reels may require additional adjustment for the extra momentum created by the heavier weight of fluorocarbon. Adjust mechanical brakes to the weight of the line and lure to maximize casting distance and minimize overruns in the line.

Fused Microfilament

Braided Monofilaments were very popular for awhile but along came a more superior product by fusing, rather than braiding, the same fibers. During this process, multiple microfilaments of gel-spun polyethylene fibers are fused together to produce what appears to be a single strand that is ultra-thin, super-strong, and very sensitive. Fused line is cheaper because it is easier to make than braided line, and has gained a significant spot in the sport fishing industry.

Spectra Fiber

Spectra fiber lines have gained a lot of acceptance among fisherman mainly due to the following reasons:

- Low Stretch
  - Spectra has very low-stretch (3% maximum) which means a fish bite is easily felt and the hook-set is quick and sure. Getting a fish away from the bottom structure is more likely, compared to monofilament stretching more than 25%.
- Small Diameter
  - A very high strength-to-diameter ratio of Spectra is attractive because:
  - More line can be put on a given reel.

- o Smaller reels may be used in a given application.
- o Greater breaking strength line may be spooled on the same reel.
- High Tensile Strength
    - o Spectra fiber is so strong that it is used in bulletproof vests; replacing Kevlar in that application. It is about 10 times as strong as steel, pound for pound. The finished line has a tensile strength of about 600,000 pounds per square inch versus monofilament which has a tensile strength of about 100,000 pounds per square inch.
- Long Life
    - o Spectra has a very long life, it does not rot, and is not readily damaged by ultraviolet rays in sunlight, as is monofilament.
    - o Not affected by water Spectra does not swell in water, nor does it lose strength when wet.
- Light Weight
    - o Spectra does not weigh you down. Stand-up fishermen really appreciate the lightweight of a spool of Spectra

Properties of Line

Most anglers do not pay enough close attention to the properties of line; if they did they would purchase line more wisely and evaluate it closely before using it. So here we are going to go over each of the properties to help you better understand and make more informed purchases next time you buy line for your reel. There are several critical properties of any line:

- breaking strength
- abrasion resistance
- diameter
- stretch
- flexibility
- knot strength
- uniformity
- visibility
- durability

Breaking Strength:
The feature that stands out the most with line is its breaking strength, that is how much pressure must be applied to an unknotted line before it will break. However this is also an area that has a lot of

disparity between products, and that is poorly understood by anglers.

There are two breaking strength categories "Test" and "Class", I'm sure you've heard of these but we will discuss them more in detail.

Class lines are mainly used by saltwater big game anglers, who are especially interested in establishing line-class world records. Class lines are guaranteed to break at or below their marked metric strength in wet condition, which is necessary to conform to the world-record specifications of the International Game and Fish Association (IGFA). Lines that conform to this standard are labeled with "class" or "IGFA class".

Any line not labeled as "class", is by definition considered "test" line. With test line there is no guarantee as to its breaking strength, it make break at, lower or higher, than the labeled strength. However most test line actually breaks higher than its strength rating, some a lot higher.

Since there is a great deal of difference in the actual breaking strength of various test lines, many anglers are actually fishing with line stronger than what they believe. Some anglers believe that a line is stronger just because it feels that it is but that not true. It is meaningless to wrap a piece of line around your wrist and pull on it, to proclaim it is stronger, that is dry strength, which is not relevant. If you actually wanted to test it, you would first have to soak the line in water for a period of time then test it.

Braided and fused line is not exception to this rule. Fluorocarbon is the one line that does not show and discernible loss in strength between wet or dry.

Diameter:

In the old days the diameter of the line was directly related to the breaking strength of the line. However monofilament line manufacturers have found ways to produce ultrathin lines that have the same breaking strength as larger conventional mono lines. In comparison a monofilament line with a 24 pound breaking strength may have the diameter of a 10 pound conventional mono line.

This creates more confusion for the angler during comparison shopping. Also anglers have had concerns that thin diameter lines have less abrasion resistance than thinner line, in conventional mono lines this may still hold true, but ultrathin monofilament lines have a high-degree of abrasion resistance.

There is a clear relationship between casting distance and line diameter when using the same weight lure, the smaller the diameter the further casting distance is achieved.

About the only other factor that you should be worried about with diameter is the amount of line that you can fit on your spool, especially if you anticipate fighting strong fish where you need the extra line.

Abrasion Resistance:

I grew up in rural Alabama, and if there is one thing you learn very quickly about it is abrasion resistance. Logs, trees, stumps, and rocks were prevalent in almost every body of water that you fished. So understanding the limitations of your line was a very important part of fishing. Although abrasion resistance is one of the most difficult qualities of line to test because there has been no laboratory test yet to be devised that can accurately test the abrasive contact that your line will come into contact with during fishing. Manufacturers claim that fused monofilament line has more abrasion resistance than nylon monofilament line however that has never been proven on the water. The experience of anglers has actually been that the abrasion resistance of microfilament lines is actually poorer than that of good quality nylon monofilament.

You can run your fingers along the first 10 inches or so of line to lure and feel any nicks, scrapes or cuts. You should do this periodically and when you feel something cut off the line just above the bad spot in the line and re-tie your lure, especially after catching a fish or hanging on a snag. It's important to remember that all line is subject to abrasion but some lines do resist abrasion better than others, the key is to find a comfortable balance between a line that provides good abrasion resistance and also maintain the other key qualities you desire.

Stretch

Most all lines will stretch, the issue is just how much do they stretch and how will this affect your fishing. Stretch has both good and bad properties, it helps forgive mistakes when fighting a fish, poor drag settings, and sudden up close strikes. Yet it hampers the inexperienced angler who does not keep the slack out of the line, is poor at feeling strikes at long distances. The average stretch in nylon monofilament line is 30% wet, that means with 5 inches of line it would stretch to almost 6.5 inches.

Microfilaments have virtually no stretch, less than 4%, and provide the angler with increased ability to detect strikes, better hook setting, more control fighting the fish, and provide better lure sensitivity. This is ideal with plastics fishing, when being able to detect the slightest tap can be important.

Anglers that use high stretch monofilament line and anglers that use low stretch microfilament lines, have to fish them differently. With microfilament line you have to be careful not to set the hook to hard or you will rip the lure out of the fish's mouth, and you must be careful that you are not fighting the fish too hard as well or you will get the same result. These can be compensated for by either loosening the drag or using a more limber rod.

Flexibility

Line must perform many functions and to do that line must have the right flexibility between being limp and stiff. A limp line is great for casting because it comes off the spool easily and straightens out quickly but it lacks sensitivity. Stiff lines decrease casting distances and are harder to manage on the spool causing backlashes. The molecular structure of nylon monofilament line is such that it forms a memory when left in a certain position for an extended period of time, such as on the spool.

TIP – You can loosen the memory on line by removing the spool from your reel and soaking it for a period of time in water so that the line will absorb some of the water and become limp again.

Braided and Fused microfilament lines are different in this respect and have very low memory, excellent castability and low stretch, wet or dry.

Knot Strength

When you are tying knots you should always consider the type of line that you are using, knots used with say fused monofilaments will not be as good with nylon monofilaments or braided line. Braided lines are especially a concern because if a knot is tied improperly the line will actually cut into itself and break with medium pressure. Also fused monofilament and braided lines is slick and will not hold good using conventional knots. The key is to know which knots work best with which types of lines and adjust accordingly.

One of the most popular knots that work great with just about every type of line is the Uni Knot. It is also fairly easy to tie in the dark with practice. The Uni Knot works well with braided lines as well as monofilament, but by far it is the best way to tie high-strength and most all small diameter braided lines.

First, run the line through the eye of the hook for several inches. Turn the end back toward the eye to form a circle as shown in illustration #1. With thumb and finger of the left hand, grasp both strands of line and the crossing strand in a single grip at the point marked just forward of the hook. Now, make six turns with the end around both strands of line and through the circle, as in illustration #2.

Maintaining the same grip with the left hand, pull on the end of the line in the direction shown by the arrow until all the wraps are snugged tight and close together. Snugging down tightly at this stage is essential for maximum knot strength. If you make six turns and snug the knot tightly, you'll get most of the line strength.

Finally, slide the finished knot tight against the eye of the hook by dropping the tag end and pulling solely on the standing part of the line as shown by the arrow in illustration #3. The excess end can be trimmed flush with the knot after final positioning, as shown in illustration #4.

Uniformity

You would have a reasonable expectation that all line will be uniform from the start of the spool to the end of the spool, and with premium line it probably will be. But those bargain line where you can buy several thousand feet for a few dollars, well that's because they might not be quite so uniform, you might have thicker weak spots or thinner strong spots, but all in all with bargain lines you can pretty much expect to get junk, so be careful and stay away from those bargain bins.

Visibility

The visibility of a line does not play any part in the performance of the line, whether it is clear, camo, or fluorescent does not change the strength, castability or abrasion resistance. It does however play a big part in what the fish thinks of the line in the water. It will depend on where you are fishing and under what conditions, is it clear and shallow? Then the visibility of the line will be more of a concern then say someone fishing in murky waters.

Anglers want a line that is as close to invisible under the water as possible but highly visible above the water. Some lines however may actually absorb light and be more visible, which can scare some fish in certain circumstances. If the line has a shiny surface it could produce a flash which will scare fish as well.

DuPont was the first line manufacturer to introduce fluorescent lines, and it was very popular in the beginning, especially for anglers who's eyes weren't quite was good as they use to be, or for fishing plastics or other bottom baits where visibility of line movement was very important. However, after years of line competitors negatively speaking of fluorescent lines causing sales to decline, DuPont let the patent run out, after it ran out the other line competitors quickly started making their own fluorescent lines.

Durability

Some manufacturers tout the durability of their fishing line as being the single most important trait. Durability however is actually a combination of all the features. Just because a line is rated with high durability does not necessary mean it is the best, it may be stronger in some areas but weaker in others. So be sure to look for a balance in all properties.

Toray's Superhard Premium-Plus Bawo HiGrade Fluorocarbon.

Regardless of the higher price tag, average of $25-$30 per spool, I still consider this my confidence line, just because I know how durable, reliable and abrasion resistant this line is. I tend to be overly picky when it comes to the gear I use and this is no exception. I have studied and conducted quite a few field tests, and the numbers don't lie, this is one of the best, if not "the best" fluorocarbon's on the market! If you haven't tried it, trust me you will love it!

Toray is the #1 selling fishing line in Japan. All lines undergo strict guidelines of Toray expert technicians and very rigorous field testing. This line is 100% Fluorocarbon and highly abrasive resistant, it can withstand even the harshest conditions without breaking down. Available in 3,4,5,6,7,8,10,12,14,16,20 LB sizes.

The Proper Care of Line

Line Twist

One of the most common problems anglers face is line twist, however anglers are too quick to blame the line they are using, when line in fact does not twist on its own but needs an outside source to cause line twist. There are several reasons that line twist can occur such as, a loose drag, using a lure without a swivel, swift currents, and a lure that is improperly adjusted.

If the cause if a faulty lure then you will need to properly adjust it so that it runs smoothly without turning over and over, also you should be using a swivel or snap ring to connect to the lure. Practically every lure that turns over or revolves will put a twist in your line.

If your drag is too loose and slips when you are fighting a fish it will cause line twist. Also if you are using spinning gear and reeling a fish in without pumping the rod you will put a bad twist in your line.

Coils

Fishing line with memory such as Nylon Monofilament will develop coils. To remove the coils you should remove the spool from the reel and soak the line in lukewarm water, this will cause the line to relax.

Another method that some use is to put tension on the line by tying the end of the line to a stationary object then backing away and raising the rod tip and pulling as if fighting a fish, does this 6-8 times.

The proper way to spool line onto your reel:

You should replace your fishing line at a minimum at least once per season; if you fish frequently then you should change it more often. I know some anglers that swear by changing their line every fishing trip, for tournament angler I would agree but for the average angler I recommend a few times a season.

1. Take the old line off the reel, then run the end of the new line up through the rod guides to the reel and tie it to the spool of the reel.

2. Put a pencil into the new spool and have somebody hold it. Or use a reel filling station that you can buy at a tackle shop to hold the spool of line. To avoid twists, make sure the line feeds off the top of the supply reel. You should also run the line through a thick book such as a phone book between the line spool and the reel spool, this will create just enough tension while

spooling the line onto your reel to create a nice uniform wrap.

3. For a bait casting reel, fill to within a quarter inch of the outer rim.

4. For a spinning reel, you place the supply reel on the floor. You need to determine whether to place it label side up, or down, in order to minimize introducing line twists during the loading process. This needs to be done for every supply reel, as the direction the line has been loaded can vary from reel to reel, even among the same brands of line. The following 3 steps detail how to determine which side of the supply reel should face up.

   a. Look down at the top of your spinning reel, and turn the handle as if you are retrieving the line. Note the direction that the bail rotates around the spool. Most spinning reels rotate in a clockwise direction.

   b. Examine your supply spool, and find the end of the line (the lead). It may be secured by tape. Orient the supply spool so that the lead is at the top and the label is facing you.

   c. If the lead is coming off the spool in a clockwise direction (i.e., if the free end of the line were an arrow, it would be point to your left), you want to place the supply reel on the floor label side up. Otherwise, you want to place it on the floor label side down. If your spinning reel turns in a counter-clockwise direction, you want to reverse this.

5. Run the end of the new line up through the rod guides to the reel, and tie onto the spool, making sure to lift the bail arm first so it will loop line on as you reel. Once the line is tied onto the spool lower the bail arm.

6. Hold the line between two fingers to keep it taut as you reel a couple of feet onto the reel.

7. Stop reeling and dip the rod toward the spool on the floor. If the line twists onto itself, turn the spool over before putting more line on. If the line is okay, go ahead and finish.

    a. For a spinning reel, a good way to spool the line is to take a soft cotton cloth and hold the line in the cloth at about the first eye. Apply a good amount of tension, so the line does not spool loose, and you can real as fast as you like.

8. Fill the reel only until it is about a quarter inch from the rim.

9. For a closed-faced reel, fill it the same way you do a spinning reel, except make sure you run the line through the hole in the reel face before tying it to the reel spool. Screw the face back on before reeling on the new line.

TIPS:

- Using a line conditioner to treat your filler spools prior to filling your reel spool will help the line wind on your reel better with less twist. Regular use of a quality line conditioner before and after fishing will protect your line and help it last longer and give you longer more accurate casts.

- To avoid loops when you fish, keep tension on the line whenever you are reeling. If you need to, hold the line between your thumb and finger in front of the reel.

- If you do get a lot of twists in your line, take the lure off and just let a lot of line out behind the boat as you go. This will take the loops out.

- If you don't have a boat, just take off the lure and tie your line to a post. Walk away, spooling out line behind you. Now have somebody cut the line free so you can reel it back on, but be sure to keep tension on it with your fingers.

- Take the old line to a line recycling bin. You can find these at most tackle shops.

- If you are using braided line, make sure you put cloth tape or a layer of mono on the reel first. Otherwise the braid will slip around the spool and you won't be able to set the hook.

- If you're a real tight-wad, you might want to take the old line off onto a different spool, then re-spool it on backwards. That way the used part is down by the bottom and fresher line is up where you use it.

- To attach the new line to the spool, you can tie a regular square knot, but make sure you get the knot snug against the spool so it doesn't slip. First aid tape on the reel spool really helps with the slippage problem.

- Closed-face reels don't hold much line, so make sure to unscrew the cover now and then to check how much you've got on there.

"Why does the line jump out of place on my reel?"
This is caused by one of two things, either your spool is too full, look to see if the line bulges past

the top of the spool if so then take some off, or you are using a line that is too heavy for the size baits you are using so that during retrieve there is not enough tension being placed on the line to properly seat it on the spool.

"Why does my line keep getting tangled?" You could have spooled it backwards. Line has memory so it needs to be spooled on the reel the same way it was spooled on the spool when you bought it. Most of the time if you lay the spool on the floor with label side up it will work.

Line and Lure Conditioners

If you're like me, in the old days we didn't pay that much attention to our fishing line, it was something that you just spooled on and checked every now and then for abrasion but that was basically it. Well back then line wasn't quite as technologically advanced as it is today and the cost wasn't near what it is today either. So anglers all over the world had to change their way of thinking and pay a lot more attention to their lines. If you think about it, that very fine thread of material is your only connection between you and your trophy fish; do you really want to be worried about whether it is performing at its best?

Fishermen are always on the lookout for anything that will give them an advantage over the fish they are after and the competition they may be fishing against. The right lure combined with the proper presentation is key to catching a fish of a lifetime or winning tournaments. Presentation is as much about your equipment working efficiently and consistently as it is about skill. For year's fisherman have relied on silicone-based treatments in an effort to reduce line drag and resistance during casting. Unfortunately these products rarely have any positive effect on today's more specialized lines and end up making hands and tackle oily and can pollute our waterways.

Line and Lure Conditioner was designed to address the problems that anglers face in working for the perfect bait presentation. Line & Lure Conditioner will add yards to your casts, reduce casting effort and virtually eliminate the frustrations of backlash and line twists. Regular use will greatly extend the life of all types of line as added benefit. All without the oily mess and pollution problems associated with oil based treatments. This all adds up to casting more accurately, more often. Now isn't that what we're all after in the first place.

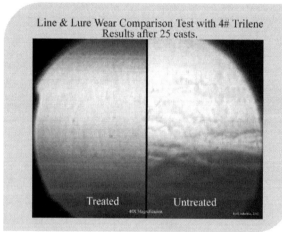

I would like to point out a few "dynamics" of our product that will help you better understand some of the benefits an angler can expect with the regular use of Line & Lure and why it is miles ahead of the others line products.

The only real commercial competition for Line & Lure is Blakemore's Reel Magic. It needs to be stated that oil based line dressings like WD-40 and

Reel Magic have been around since the 1950's and were used to address some of the problems that anglers were experiencing with monofilament line, the predominant line of the time.

Reel Magic and WD-40 is merely silicone oil with added petroleum distillates that are listed as toxic by the EPA and on the product's label. The silicone oil adds some level of lubrication to line but is very temporary. Just how temporary these products are, can easily be observed when casting after a fresh application. One will plainly see the oil slick it leaves on the water surface. We anglers love the waterways that we fish, so why would we use or condone the use of toxic products that wash into lakes, rivers and bays?

Reel Magic and WD-40 does have a relaxing effect on the corkscrew memory that we see in monofilament line due to the petroleum solvents added to it. Unfortunately, these solvents reduce memory by literally dissolving the outer surface of the line, thereby weakening it. The use of these products, can contribute up to a 50 % loss of monofilament's line strength in just a few days. If that wasn't bad enough, these oils and solvents sprayed onto reel spools are also getting into the reel's moving parts including bearings, gears and seals. The very nature of the oil in these products draws and holds dirt to these parts, negatively affecting their performance and lifespan. The solvents in the products are known to degrade the seals that the manufacturer built into the reel to protect the inner moving parts. Ask any professional reel repair technician and chances are that he will agree.

On the other hand, Line & Lure contains a blend of non-toxic, polymers that are not found in any other "fishing line dressing or line conditioner".

"Line & Lure makes my line last longer, my casting effortless and more accurate. Try it I know you will agree." – Bill Dance

The proprietary polymer blend in Line & Lure imparts a coating to line that actually bonds to the line's surface. In theory, this bond becomes a permanent part of the line. The only way to remove this coating is to abrade it from the line, by friction. The polymers fill any line surface imperfections and create a very uniform and smooth microscopic coating on the line. This smooth surface is inherently more resistant to friction than an untreated one. In this case, this phenomenon provides multiple benefits.

Fishing Reel Care and Maintenance 101 | 189

First, as friction does start to attack the line (as it goes through the rod guides, over obstacles, etc.), the polymer acts as a sacrificial buffer to that friction. Practically, our replaceable polymer finish wears instead of the line itself. This of course extends the line's life tremendously.

Checkout the Saltwater Line & Lure

Secondarily, these polymers are extremely hydrophobic, meaning that they literally push water away at the molecular level. This hydrophobic action reduces the amount of water that is retained on the line during a retrieve. It is this water surface tension on the reel spool that is a major contributor to casting distance restriction. This phenomenon is further demonstrated when we take into consideration the reduction in backlash that anglers find when using Line & Lure with bait casting reels.

This surface tension principle is the same thing that one experience when they pick up a sweating drinking glass and find the coaster being picked up with the glass. The less water on the line, the less the resistance caused by surface tension. This equals much longer casts and fewer backlashes!

It is also easy to see that with less water retention on the line there will be less contaminants coming

Roland Martin uses Line & Lure

back up on to the reel. This is especially important when fishing in saltwater. As we all know, it is the salt crystals that form in-between the loops of line on reels that cause a lot of the wear damage to fishing line. This salt also invades the seals on reels and over time acts like sandpaper wearing on reel components. Just as on the line, the polymers in line & Lure protect the seals from the elements, helping keeping them in prime condition. The anticorrosive properties of Line & Lure also dramatically reduce corrosion damage to rod, reel and artificial bait surfaces. Simply put, Line & Lure greatly extends the useful life of fishing equipment, lines and baits.

Fishing Reel Care and Maintenance 101 | 191

Line and lure contains extremely high sunscreen protection. This sunscreen blocks the UV rays from sunlight. UV radiation has a massively destructive effect on fishing line. Fishing line can literally burn at about half the rate as unprotected human skin! Using Line & Lure on your line is equivalent to using an SPF 30 on your skin. The competition has no more UV protection then baby oil. Anglers are very happy with the benefits that they get using Line & Lure on monofilament line, but please keep in mind that Line & Lure was primarily designed by Kevin Van Dam and RMR Industries to address the inherent problems anglers experience with fluorocarbon, co-polymers and braided lines. Other line dressings have little or no positive effect on these hi-tech lines.

After 1-½ years in development and testing by thousands of anglers around the world, Line and Lure has been proven to work effectively on any type of line made by any manufacturer. In addition, it is the only line conditioner that positively affects the flexibility, knot strength, casting and control of fluorocarbon line. Anglers using Line & Lure can expect the following benefits:

* Longer casts.......guaranteed!
* Virtually eliminates line memory, backlash, tangles, and twists
* Restores new line performance to old tired line
* Fights saltwater corrosion on reels, rods and tackle
* Leaves no oily residues or scents like other line treatments

* Contains no polluting petroleum distillates as in other conditioners
* Fights fading and damage to gear with high sunscreen
* Reduces water spotting on electronics & sunglasses
* Environmentally safe - non-toxic

* Superior Fly Line Dressing
* Unsurpassed de-icing performance in ice fishing

Cryogenic Treatment

Cryogenics has been around for a long time, and no I'm not talking Star Trek and freezing a human body which is actually called Cryonics. NASA has been using cryogenically treated parts in satellites for years. NASA discovered that by super-freezing metals that there was a molecular change that occurred which would actually double or triple the lifetime of a part. For years this technology was out of reach for the average person and only used for government applications. That's not true today, this same technology is now available to extend the lifetime for your reels, line and other equipment.

Deep Cryogenic Treatment (DCT) involves the cooling of metals and other materials to very low temperatures, typically around -190°C. Liquid nitrogen (boiling point -196°C) is usually used to achieve this although other liquefied gasses can be used to reach even lower temperatures (for example, neon, boiling point -246°C).

Early experiments with cryogenic treatment - America's Los Alamos nuclear weapons laboratory built a cryogenic facility as early as 1952 - plunged the component to be treated straight into the liquid coolant, with the result that many were damaged because of thermal shock. Today's DCT equipment is computer controlled so that components are cooled and warmed slowly either side of the 'soak' period over which the minimum temperature is retained. Typically cach phase of the process takes many hours, and although liquid nitrogen is still used it never comes into direct contact with whatever is being treated. Instead it is usually dripped into the cryogenic chamber where it evaporates and cools the contents indirectly.

DCT's effects have been most widely studied in the context of engineering steels, where it is used to complete the heat treatment process. The properties of many steels can be enhanced by first heating them to about 900°C and then rapidly quenching (cooling) them in water or oil. The metallurgy of this process is well understood. Heating has the effect of transforming the steel into a soft solid phase called austenite; on rapid quenching most - typically 85% - of this is converted into a much harder form called martensite, which is responsible for the quenched steel's enhanced hardness. Increased brittleness is an undesirable side effect but subsequent tempering - raising the steel's temperature to between 200 and 600'C and then cooling it in air - can offset this, and restore both ductility and toughness (the ability of the material to resist cracking).

The problem with this process is that the conversion from austenite to martensite is incomplete, which results in internal stresses that can weaken the metal and compromise its dimensional stability. What DCT does, in effect, is complete the quenching process so that most of the retained austenite - the source of the internal stresses - is converted to martensite. The benefits can be dramatic. When DCT is used to treat tool steels, for instance, tool life is typically improved by 200-400%, sometimes 600%.

Although DCT's effect on steel is the most completely understood, the technique is also quite widely applied to other metals such as east iron, titanium, aluminum and brass, and to non-metallic materials such as plastics. In this case the improvement in physical properties apparently results from the elimination of dislocations in the material's microstructure.

The process is simple, the metal parts are super-cooled down to -192°C (-316°F) and held there for 2 days, then they go off for final touches in a tempering oven. The treatment does not change the hardness of the metal, and does not change its shape in any way. I have been told that this process works with every type of metal including aluminum and magnesium, and even plastics, nylon and other materials.

So how does cryogenics relate to fishing reels?

For most people the only association they have regarding fish and ultra-low temperatures involves a box of fish sticks. Without diminishing The Groton's Fisherman or his fine products, there is indeed a freezing process involving not fish but fishing equipment.

Cryogenic processing is a scientific technique that employ's temperatures in the range of minus 300 degrees Fahrenheit. Subjecting various materials to very low temperatures in a very controlled, methodical manner causes molecular changes that produce positive results for the use of these materials.

Monofilament fishing line produced from nylon polymer has a problem with curl memory. Make a great cast and there's most of your line in spring-like curls across the surface of the water. The line spends most of its life wound around its reel. Take it off the reel and it still wants to return to its previous circular wound shape.

By freezing this line at minus 316 degrees Fahrenheit for 32 hours the molecular structure is drastically altered. These molecular changes cause the line to be smoother and the stresses that were imparted to the line during manufacturing are relieved. The curl memory is practically erased. Another result of the freezing process is greater wear resistance, making the line simply last longer.

Depending on the polymer and its physical characteristics, the line can also show an increase in tensile strength of up to 50 percent.

Those fishermen who are saltwater anglers frequently find their reels have problems with the effects of saltwater on the mechanical components. Commonly this problem is basically corrosion caused by a reaction of the metal parts to marine salt. On steel this would be known as rust but on brass, aluminum, magnesium and stainless, the materials the internal reel components are made from, it is a grey-white powder like substance that results in pitting, locked and sheared gears, abnormal wear and aggravation.

The cryogenic process applied to saltwater fishing equipment will reduce the corrosive reaction the metallic surfaces have when subjected to seawater. The smoother and tighter molecular structure resists corrosion and wear, resulting in greater use life, smoother reel operation, less money spent on repairs and more satisfaction from your fishing experience. Whether we call it rust or corrosion, it still means the same thing: the elements are literally eating up the materials. Cryogenic processing is a great way to keep your favorite reel casting out and reeling them in.

Besides an occasional sharpening, hooks don't get much attention. There are lots of fish lost to worn barbs, corroded hooks and dull points. The easy fix for hook problems is cryogenic processing. Reducing the effects of rusting and corrosion as well as making hooks stay sharp longer will certainly put the odds in your favor. Besides, we all know how corrosive worm guts are on hooks.

Other water sports related items that gain significant results by cryogenic processing include props, boat motor components (NASCAR engines are commonly cryogenically processed), drive line components, and hardware exposed to salt air and water.

Cryogenic processing is a technique discovered by NASA scientists several years back. The actual technique for properly and successfully applying the cryogenic process has been plagued with problems. As with any new science, it takes research, experimentation and quantification. The science of the cryogenic process has been no different. Only in the last ten years has reliable cryogenic processing come of age. Now cryogenic results are consistent, uniform, reliable, readily available and cost effective. Researchers in Japan, Russia, China, Ireland and the USA have now refined a process that at one time seemed more prone to snake-oil than science into a practical way to apply basic physics to improve the lives of everyone including those who just want to catch a fish.

For more information please contact, Down River Cryogenics-West at Hayden, Idaho by calling 208-651-6500 ask for Terry Thompson or Ron Moffatt

Editor's Tip
Cryogenically treated fishing line also increases the breaking strength of the line, so this method is not recommended for "Class" Lines.

THINGS YOU SHOULD KNOW

1. AGE OF PENN REEL BY COLOR OF ORIGINAL HANDLE
Amber = 30-40's
Red = 50's
Green = 60's
White = 70's
Black = 80's
Rubber = 90's

2. THE TRUTH ABOUT WD-40 AND WHAT YOU SHOULD KNOW.
WD-40 is not really a lubricant, "WD" stands for Water Displacement" and 40 because it was the 40th attempt by the chemist to perfect it. It also does not contain any "Fish Oils" as has been a myth floating around for quite some time. The Environmental Protection Agency states that they do not recommend the use of this substance as a bait additive and class it as a pollutant. If it was over used on a fishery by several anglers it could have an adverse impact on the aquatic environment with some fish and invertebrates suffering. In very small amounts it should not harm fish, but it is impossible to say at this moment what levels would be damaging. Using WD40 on your baits could leave you liable to prosecution. Even though it has been known to be used by some catfishermen as an attractant, it is a pollutant to our lakes and rivers.

3. DETERMINING GEAR RATIO BY NUMBER OF TEETH
You can tell the gear ratio of any reel by counting the number of teeth on the main drive gear and the pinion gear. In a typical setup with 53 teeth of the pinion gear and 10 teeth on the main drive gear, this would be a 5.3:1 ratio since the pinion will turn 5.3 times for each full revolution of the main drive gear.

4. HOW MANY FISHERMEN ARE THERE IN THE UNITED STATES?

In 2006 there were an estimated 8.5 million saltwater anglers and 25 million freshwater anglers, in the United States, with the major of saltwater anglers Florida and Texas. In Alaska more average persons fish than anywhere else, 1 out of 3 people fish in Alaska.

INSIDE THE NUMBERS

• More Americans fish than play golf (24.4 million) and tennis (10.4 million) combined.

• If fishing were ranked as a corporation, it would be 47 on the 2007 Fortune 500 list of America's largest companies based on total sales. That's well ahead of such global giants as Microsoft or Time Warner.

• At nearly 40 million, the number of American anglers is more than 33 times the average attendance per game at all Major League baseball parks combined.

• The more than one million jobs supported by anglers are almost three times the number of people who work for United Parcel Service in the U.S.

• The National Sporting Goods Association ranked fishing sixth out of 42 recreation activities, preceded only by walking, swimming, exercising, camping and bowling.

IS YOUR BOAT PROTECTED?

Normally it would seem strange to find information on protecting your boat in a reel care and maintenance book but I strongly feel that your boat is just as much a valuable asset to your fishing as your reels are. *If you are spending countless unneeded hours maintaining your boat then that is time that could be better spent maintaining your reels.* I have personally used BTS Protectant from RMR Industries and I guarantee you it is the best boat care product on the market, these guys know what they are doing. *This is a revolutionary product that is changing the way anglers care for and maintain their boats; believe me when I say if you aren't using it, you aren't protected!* - Jeff Holder

BTS Protectant is the industry's first one step all surface conditioning protectant that safeguards your valuable marine investments from the costly damage caused by exposure to the elements as well as the unpleasant effects of environmental contamination including, mold and mildew staining and related odors. The BTS Formula was created as a time saving "all in one" conditioner/protectant specifically developed for the harsh environmental conditions of the Florida coast where sun, salt corrosion and mold and mildew cost consumers millions of dollars in property damage yearly.

BTS Protection is long lasting; retreat every few months, not every week or every outing as with other products. The oil free formula is not slippery and will not stain other materials that it may come into contact with.

BTS Protectant's polymer technology leaves no chalky build-up like waxes that require application in the shade and during cool temperatures. BTS can be applied in direct sunlight with minimal effort and dries in minutes. Unlike spray and shine preparations that suggestion application after every outing, BTS will provide superior protection with occasional use. Regular cleaning is made easy with BTS and without the need for other cleaning products.

Once applied, the special "polymers" seal and protect the treated surfaces, allowing for an easy clean up with a damp cloth. BTS can be used to protect and beautify virtually all surfaces including fiberglass, gel coat, plastic, metal, carpet, vinyl, leather, painted surfaces and wood. BTS is ideal for keeping vinyl upholstery soft, supple and looking "showroom" new for years. Gel coat staining from dirty water, engine exhaust, as well as insects are a thing of the past with the regular use of BTS. BTS adds a water and soil repellant finish to boat covers and canvas. Plastic windows will stay clearer and last years longer with BTS protection.

Reel Service & Parts Directory

This reel service and parts supply directory will provide you with a list of reputable business that can provide parts for all your servicing needs. You can also visit us online at www.reelschematic.com

The Reel Doctor

Providing services and repairs for reels, rods, trolling motors, and underwater cameras
8732 – 51 Avenue
Edmonton, AB
T6E 5E8
Canada
Inside Canada – 1.866.431.0146
Outside Canada – 1.780.431.0146
service@reeldr.com
www.reeldr.com

Bucko's Tackle Service

Reel Parts and Service
191 Stafford Road
Fall River, MA 02721
1.508.674.7900
mjbucko@mindspring.com
www.buckosparts.com

JL Reel Service

Reel Parts and Service
910 N. Washington Avenue
Madison, SD 57042
605.256.4431
www.jlreelservice.com

Bay Area Reel Service

Reel Servicing and Repair
11201 Linden Lane
Port Richey, FL 34668
1.813.728.5865
www.bayareareelservice.com

Tom White Rod & Reel Repair

1024 New Scotland Road
Albany, New York 12208
1.518.488.9094
twhite10@nycap.rr.com
www.fishing-reel-repair.com

Mike's Reel Repair

#108-31060 Peardonville Road
Abbotsford, BC, Canada V2T6K5
1.888.404.1119
www.mikereelrepair.com

Dave's Reel Service

602 Avon Court
Vernon Hills, IL 60061
1.847.549.7170
repair@davesreelservice.com
www.davesreelservice.com

Anglers Parts Can

Large Supply of Reel Parts
Box 571
Sun Prairie, WI 53590
1.608.225.5501
www.anglerspartscan.com

Vintage Reels

The Old Reel Collectors Association (ORCA)
www.orcaonline.org

FOR BEARING REPLACEMENTS FOR REELS:

Warranty Service

Abu-Garcia Reels

Abu Garcia warrants to the original purchaser that its tackle products are free from defects in materials or workmanship for a period of one (1) year from the date of purchase. If a product proves defective in some way, return it prepaid and with proof of the date of purchase, to:

Abu Garcia /Pure Fishing
Attn: Angler Service
1900 18th Street Spirit Lake,
IA 51360

In the case of fishing rods please include $9.95 to cover return postage and handling. If after inspection, we determine that the product was defective in material or workmanship, we shall, at our option, repair or replace it without charge. We are not responsible for normal wear and tear, for equipment used commercially or for failures caused by accidents, abuse, alteration, modification, misuse or improper care.

There are no other express warranties beyond the terms of this limited warranty. In no event shall any implied warranties, including merchantability and fitness for a particular purpose, extend beyond the duration of the express warranty contained herein. In no event shall

Berkley/Pure Fishing be liable for incidental or consequential damages.

Some states do not allow limitations on how long an implied warranty lasts or the exclusion of limitation of incidental or consequential damages, so the above limitations or exclusions may not apply to you. This warranty gives you specific rights and you may have other rights which vary from state to state.

Accurate Reels

How Long Does The Limited Warranty Coverage Last? This limited warranty runs for a period of five (5) years starting from the date that the ATD reel was first purchased by the consumer. Coverage terminates if you sell or otherwise transfer the reel.

What Does The Limited Warranty Cover? Accurate Fishing Products warrants to the original purchaser that its ATD fishing reels are free from defects in material and workmanship with the exceptions stated below. Accurate Fishing Products will also, free of charge, lubricate your ATD reel one (1) time per year during the term of this Limited Warranty.

What Is Not Covered By This Limited Warranty? This limited warranty does not cover damage or problems caused by misuse, abuse, neglect, accident, installation, alterations or failure to properly maintain the reel.

What Will Accurate Fishing Products Do? Accurate Fishing Products will repair or replace any reel which is defective in material or workmanship covered by this limited warranty at no charge. Accurate Fishing Products will also, free of charge, lubricate your ATD reel one (1) time per year during the term of this Limited Warranty.

How Do You Get Service? If something goes wrong with your reel, or you want to receive the annual lubrication service, send it to Accurate Fishing Products, postage pre-paid, along with a sales receipt or other proof of the date of purchase. Be sure to include a short note explaining the problem.

Send the ATD reel to Accurate Fishing Products at:
Accurate Fishing Products
Warranty Repairs
807 E. Parkridge Avenue
Corona, California 92879
1-888-ACCU-372

Please pack your reel with all parts that have been removed securely in a sturdy box. Be certain that your package is adequately insured and mailed with a shipping company that has tracking capabilities. Be sure to include your name, address and telephone number. Accurate Fishing Products will inspect your reel and contact you within 30 days of receipt to inform you whether the problem is covered by this limited warranty. There is no charge for the inspection.

What Are The Warranty Limitations And Limitations Of Liability? There are no other express warranties. Any warranty of merchantability or fitness for a particular purpose is limited to the duration of this limited warranty. Accurate Fishing Products shall NOT be liable for any loss of use, loss of time, inconvenience, commercial loss, or other incidental or consequential damages. Some states do not allow limitations on how long an implied warranty lasts, or the exclusion or limitation of incidental or consequential damages, so the above limitations and exclusions may not apply to you. This limited warranty gives you specific legal rights, you may have additional rights which vary from state to state.

Avet Reels

Avet Reels one year Limited Warranty

Avet Reels, Inc. warrants to the original purchaser that this product will be free from defects in materials and workmanship for a period of one year from the date of purchase. This warranty does not cover damage or malfunctions caused by accident, abuse or normal expected wear. It will be considered VOID if the reel has been subjected to damage by the owner's failure to provide necessary maintenance. If your Avet reel has a defect within the terms of the warranty, you should return it to us, postage pre-paid, to:

> Avet Reels, Inc.
> 9687 Topanga Cyn. Pl.
> Chatsworth, CA 91311.

In addition, please provide a short explanation of the problem you are experiencing with the product. We shall repair or replace the reel, at our option, without any further cost to you, including free return transportation. However, if the repair is not covered by the provisions of this warranty, Avet will perform the repair and return with a claim to you for labor, parts and return shipping charge.

Warranty Service Information

All warranties which may be implied by operation of law, including, but not limited to, warranties of fitness for any particular purpose, shall be limited to one year from the date of purchase. In no event shall Avet Reels, Inc. be liable for incidental or consequential damages for breach of this warranty or any other warranty which may be implied by law. Some states do not allow limitations on how long an implied warranty lasts, and some states do not allow the exclusion of incidental or consequential damages, so the above limitation and/or exclusion may not apply to you.

This warranty gives you specific legal rights, and you may also have other rights which vary from state to state.

Daiwa Reels

Q. Where do I send my Daiwa rod and reel for repair and service?

A. You may send your reel to any of Daiwa's Authorized Warranty Centers or to our North American Service Center. Please check the following link for the nearest Daiwa Service Center. You must send your rod directly to our North American Service Center:

Daiwa Corporation
North American Service Center
12851 Midway Place
Cerritos, CA 90703
(562) 802-9589

Q. How do I file a warranty claim?

A. Daiwa will repair or replace without charge any Daiwa rod or reel which is defective in workmanship or materials within one year from the date of purchase by the consumer. Please retain your sales slip as proof of purchase date in the event warranty work becomes necessary. Please follow these instructions when returning rods or reels for warranty repair:

Do not remove parts

Enclose proof of purchase and a statement of warranty claim with nature of problem. Also, please list the model name and number of reel/rod and your return address.

To protect against loss or damage in transit, your reel/rod should be carefully packaged and adequately insured. Please retain all shipping receipts.

Q. How long does it normally take for repair?

A. The average turnaround time for warranty and chargeable repair once payment is received is approximately 3-5 working days. It may vary depending on seasonal demand.

Q. How much does a non-warranty repair cost and how do I pay for it?

A. In order to provide the cost of repair we must examine the product. Please follow these instructions when returning rods or reels for repair:

Do not remove parts

State the nature of the problem. Also, please list the model name and number of reel/rod, and your return address.

To protect against loss or damage in transit, your reel/rod should be carefully packaged and adequately insured. Please retain all shipping receipts.

Once we examine your rod or reel we will forward an estimate to you.

Q. How do I order parts for my Daiwa reel?

A. You can order parts on line, by phone, or by mail. You may pay by credit card, check or money order, or COD.

Fin-Nor Reels

It is the goal of W.C. Bradley Co./Zebco Holdings to provide you with the very best customer service possible. However, not all products previously manufactured under the name Fin-Nor will continue to be supported from either a new build or service stand point.

Items no longer supported are:
PRIMEO: 1000, 2000, 3000, 4000
ESTIMA: ES50UL, ES100 - ES600
FIN-ITE: F201 - F304
FIN-NOR LITE: S50UL, S100 - S600
QUESTLITE: QL1000 - QL4000
QUESTLITE GOLD: QLG1000 - QLG4000
INSHORE: ISX2000 - ISX6000
STEEL RIVER: SR1000 - SR4000
TYCOON: TYS7-1 through TYS7-4, TYS5-100 through TYS5-400

The following products will be supported from a service standpoint. Service support on each of these items presents differing opportunities by model, thus we have developed item-specific service programs for each model in this list. Please contact us to learn more about the service program that is unique to your Fin-nor product.

Support programs ARE available on these products:
AHAB: 8A, 12A, 16A, 20A, LD12 - LD80-2
FIN-ITE/FIN-ITE II: 23CL - 1012

Warranty Service Information

MEGA LITE: ML1000 - ML4000
BIG GAME TROLLING: 120FNSP, 120FNSTD, 120FTRI, 25FNA - 90FNA, 50FLN, 60WFNA, 75FNA

When returning your Fin-Nor product, the following information is required to process the service:
1. Provide your Name and Address, telephone, fax number or e-mail address.
2. Properly package the product so there is no further damage during shipping.
3. Insure the package and send it pre-paid to the Fin-Nor Repair Department. (No COD shipments will be accepted)
4. To expedite the repair, give a credit card number in your description letter.
5. Check or money order is also acceptable.
6. Any charges incurred will include freight charges.

All packages should be shipped to our facility:
Fin-Nor Repair Department
6505 Tower Lane
Claremore, OK 74019-4429

NOTE: Repairs will be returned via UPS, unless other arrangements are made prior to shipment. We will not ship to a P.O. Box, please provide a UPS delivery address (street address).

Any repairs not paid for will be disposed of after 30 days from the date listed on the notification letter.

Hardy Reels

Original User Lifetime Warranty Information

All other non carbon-fibre rods and all reels manufactured by House of Hardy are covered by our Original User Lifetime Warranty against material or manufacturing defects. Our other products, excluding leaders, tippet material and other consumables, carry our original user warranty of 12 months from date of purchase. This warranty applies to products that have been used in the manner that was intended. It does not cover normal wear and tear, or apply to products that have been neglected, altered or abused in anyway, nor to any consequential loss, relating to any defect. This warranty is given in addition to your statutory rights.

Okuma Reels

http://www.okumafishingteam.com/misc/warranty.html

U.S.A. Contact Information
U.S. Head Office
OKUMA FISHING TACKLE CORP.
2310 E. Locust Court, Ontario CA 91761
Tel: 909-923-2828
Fax: 909-923-2909
1-800-GO-OKUMA, 1-800-466-5862

For **parts and service issues,** please contact:
service@okumafishing.com

Pinnacle Reels

WARRANTY AND SERVICE

Your Pinnacle/Silstar fishing product carries a limited warranty for a period of one year from the date of purchase against defects in workmanship and or materials.

During this period, Silstar Corporation of America, Inc. will perform repairs or
effect replacement, at its option. The warranty extends only to the original (Consumer) owner with valid proof of purchase. The Original warranty is non-transferable.

Purchaser should return defective rod and/or reel postage prepaid, insured with valid proof of purchase (indicating the date purchased) with $15.00 to cover return postage payable to Silstar Corporation of America, Inc. This warranty will be *VOID* if the rod or reel is found to have been subject to unauthorized alterations, abuse or damaged by failure to provide necessary and reasonable maintenance.

Retailers and wholesale outlets for Pinnacle products are NOT authorized to perform warranty repairs or exchange on behalf of Pinnacle/Silstar. Pinnacle / Silstar reels and rods not covered by warranty may be repaired at nominal charge provided these reels and rods are returned postage prepaid. We reserve the right to replace a discontinued model with a current comparable model of our choosing. This warranty gives you specific legal rights, and you may also have other rights which vary from state to state.

SHIPPING INSTRUCTIONS

All reels and rods sent in for repair or warranty service should be carefully packed and insured. Please include your name, return address, telephone number, E-mail address where you can be reached, **$15.00** check made to **Silstar Corporation**, Inc. to cover return postage, along with detailed information on the nature of the problem.

Send the Product to:

Pinnacle / Silstar Consumer Warranty & Service Center
3142 Platt Springs Rd.
Springdale, SC 29170

Phone : (888) 794-2221
Fax :   (803) 794-2252
Email :   service@pinnaclefishing.com

Penn Reels

Penn Limited Warranty: Penn Fishing Tackle Mfg. Co. warrants its Products to be free from defects in materials and workmanship for a period of one year from the date of purchase. This warranty does not cover damage or malfunctions caused by accident, abuse, or normal expected wear. If your Penn Product has a defect within the terms of the warranty you can return it to Old Inlet Bait and Tackle or Penn to be replaced or repaired. All shipping and insurance costs and transportation arrangements will be borne by you and are your responsibility. Penn will repair or replace the Product, at their option, without further cost to you (including free return transportation and insurance). If, however, the repair is not covered by the provisions of the warranty, your Penn Product will be repaired and returned to you at a reasonable charge for labor, parts and return transportation and insurance.

Carefully package and send your reels to:
FACTORY REPAIR SERVICE
PENN FISHING TACKLE
3028 W. HUNTING PARK AVE.
PHILADELPHIA, PA 19132

We recommend you send your reels to Penn via UPS so that the shipment can be tracked and we can verify receipt of your goods.

Penn Information Form:
To facilitate the processing of your reels, please fill out

a Penn Repair Information Form and include it with your shipment.

Include your name and address, and a way (or ways) for us to contact you, either by phone or email. Provide the best time to contact you, either at home or at work. You should include your credit card number, expiration date, name on card and type of card. This will help speed up your transaction. If you do not include your credit card information, we will contact you when your reels arrive at Penn, and get all necessary credit card information before we begin working on your reels.

CREDIT CARDS ONLY.

If you require an estimate, you must note this on the "special instructions" section of the repair form or in your correspondence. If you do not require an estimate and all of the required information is provided, your reel will be entered into our system and the following charges will be applied to your credit card once the repair is complete:

Quantum Reels

Quantum products are warranted for a period of one (1) year from **date of original retail purchase** against defects in workmanship and/or materials. Purchaser should return defective products postage prepaid, insured with proof of purchase direct to Quantum at 6105 E. Apache, Tulsa, OK 74115. Quantum will repair or replace products at its option and return direct to purchaser.

This warranty does not cover Quantum products damaged due to abuse, misuse, normal wear, or excessive wear caused by neglect of cleaning and lubrication required or general service requirements due to owner's failure to provide reasonable and necessary maintenance.

Quantum products not covered by the Quantum Limited Warranty may be repaired at a nominal charge to the purchaser, provided parts are available and the product is returned with return postage prepaid.

"ALL INCIDENTAL AND/OR CONSEQUENTIAL DAMAGES ARE EXCLUDED FROM THIS WARRANTY INSERT. IMPLIED WARRANTIES ARE LIMITED TO THE LIFE OF THIS WARRANTY. SOME STATES DO NOT ALLOW LIMITATIONS ON HOW LONG AN IMPLIED WARRANTY LASTS OR THE EXCLUSION OR LIMITATION OF INCIDENTAL OR CONSEQUENTIAL DAMAGES, SO THE ABOVE LIMITATIONS OR EXCLUSIONS MAY NOT APPLY TO YOU. THIS

WARRANTY GIVES YOU SPECIFIC LEGAL RIGHTS, AND YOU MAY ALSO HAVE OTHER LEGAL RIGHTS WHICH MAY VARY FROM STATE TO STATE."

The warranties described herein shall be the sole and exclusive warranties granted by Quantum and shall be the sole and exclusive remedy available to the purchaser. Correction of defects, in the manner and time period described herein, shall constitute complete fulfillment of all liabilities and responsibilities of Quantum to the purchaser with regard to this product, and shall constitute full satisfaction of all claims, whether based on contract, negligence, strict liability or otherwise. Quantum shall not be liable or in any way responsible for any damages or defects caused by repairs or attempted repairs performed by anyone other than an authorized servicer. Nor shall Quantum be liable, or in any way responsible, for any incidental or consequential property damage. Quantum reserves the right to amend or change this warranty at any time.

THIS WARRANTY GIVES YOU SPECIFIC LEGAL RIGHTS, AND YOU MAY ALSO HAVE OTHER LEGAL RIGHTS WHICH MAY VARY FROM STATE TO STATE.

The provisions of this Warranty are in addition to, and not a modification of, or a subtraction from, the statutory warranties and other rights and remedies contained in any applicable legislation. To the extent that any provision of this Warranty is inconsistent with any applicable law, such provision shall be deemed voided or amended as necessary, to comply with such law.

Shakespeare

Your new Shakespeare product comes with a limited warranty for a period of one year against defects in material and/or workmanship. Shakespeare will have no other obligation and will not be liable for incidental or consequential damages. Shakespeare makes no implied warranty of MERCHANTABILITY OR FITNESS for any period beyond the duration of each limited warranty. This warranty does not cover damage caused by addition to or alteration of the product, accident, abuse or normal wear. This warranty does not extend to products, which are put to commercial or rental use.

Some state laws do not allow exclusion of incidental or consequential damages or limitation of the duration of implied warranties, so the above exclusion and limitations might not apply to you. This warranty gives you specific rights, which vary, from state to state.

Parts & Repair
The decision to repair or replace reels under warranty will be made by the Service Center. Rods under warranty will always be replaced. Shakespeare Service Center no longer repairs any fishing rods. Shakespeare reel which are no longer covered by warranty may be repaired at a nominal charge plus shipping and handling. Call the service center for details.

Old reels
Shakespeare has been in business for more than one hundred years. We retain parts and schematics for all

reels that are six years old or less. Occasionally we may have parts for older models. Please call the Service Center for more information.

Instructions for Warranty Service
Send rods, freight prepaid and insured, to the Shakespeare Service Center at 3801 Westmore Drive Columbia SC 29223 , along with a note stating how the item was broken or damaged. Include name, mailing address, phone number, proof of date of purchase, and $7.50 for return postage and handling. For one piece rods 6'6" or longer, include an additional $2.50 for oversize fee.

Send reels, freight prepaid and insured, to the Shakespeare Service Center, along with a note stating how the item was broken or damaged. Include name, mailing address, phone number, proof of date of purchase, and $6.50 for return postage and handling.

Shakespeare will repair or replace the product at its option and return directly to the purchaser.

All authorized repairs are made by the Shakespeare Service Center in Columbia, SC. Canadian customers contact:

Rockey's Tackle Repair
10 Brammer Drive
Orillia, Ontario L3V 7T4
Canada
705-325-3526

Shimano Reels

Shimano warrants to the original purchaser that this product will be free from non-conformities in material or workmanship for the period of one year from the date of purchase.

To request repairs (or non-warranty service) send your reel, postage pre-paid, to the Shimano Authorized Warranty Center nearest you. Retailers and wholesale outlets are not required or authorized to perform warranty repairs or exchanges on behalf of Shimano. If sending your reel to Shimano directly, please call for verification on due date as some seasons experience high volume.

All warranty requests must be accompanied by a dated sales receipt, your name, address, telephone number (daytime), email address (optional), and a brief description of the issues related to your warranty request.

The following items will not be covered under warranty:
Non- ARB Ball Bearings, Roller Bearings

Zebco Reels

Zebco products are warranted for a period of one (1) year from date of original retail purchase against defects in workmanship and/or materials. Purchaser should return defective products postage prepaid, insured with proof of purchase direct to Zebco at 6105 E. Apache, Tulsa, OK 74115. Zebco will repair or replace products at its option and return direct to purchaser.

This warranty does not cover Zebco products damaged due to abuse, misuse, normal wear, or excessive wear caused by neglect of cleaning and lubrication required or general service requirements due to owner's failure to provide reasonable and necessary maintenance.

Zebco products not covered by the Zebco Limited Warranty may be repaired at a nominal charge to the purchaser, provided parts are available and the product is returned with return postage prepaid.

"ALL INCIDENTAL AND/OR CONSEQUENTIAL DAMAGES ARE EXCLUDED FROM THIS WARRANTY INSERT. IMPLIED WARRANTIES ARE LIMITED TO THE LIFE OF THIS WARRANTY. SOME STATES DO NOT ALLOW LIMITATIONS ON HOW LONG AN IMPLIED WARRANTY LASTS OR THE EXCLUSION OR LIMITATION OF INCIDENTAL OR CONSEQUENTIAL DAMAGES, SO THE ABOVE LIMITATIONS OR EXCLUSIONS MAY NOT APPLY TO YOU. THIS WARRANTY GIVES YOU SPECIFIC LEGAL RIGHTS, AND YOU MAY ALSO HAVE OTHER LEGAL RIGHTS WHICH MAY VARY FROM STATE TO STATE."

The warranties described herein shall be the sole and exclusive warranties granted by Zebco and shall be the sole and exclusive remedy available to the purchaser. Correction of defects, in the manner and time period described herein, shall constitute complete fulfillment of all liabilities and responsibilities of Zebco to the purchaser with regard to this product, and shall constitute full satisfaction of all claims, whether based on contract, negligence, strict liability or otherwise. Zebco shall not be liable or in any way responsible for any damages or defects caused by repairs or attempted repairs performed by anyone other than an authorized servicer. Nor shall Zebco be liable, or in any way responsible, for any incidental or consequential property damage. Zebco reserves the right to amend or change this warranty at any time.

THIS WARRANTY GIVES YOU SPECIFIC LEGAL RIGHTS, AND YOU MAY ALSO HAVE OTHER LEGAL RIGHTS WHICH MAY VARY FROM STATE TO STATE.

The provisions of this Warranty are in addition to, and not a modification of, or a subtraction from, the statutory warranties and other rights and remedies contained in any applicable legislation. To the extent that any provision of this Warranty is inconsistent with any applicable law, such provision shall be deemed voided or amended as necessary, to comply with such law.

A

ABEC, 24, 25, 26, 28, 29
ABEC Ratings, 24
Abrasion Resistance, 170
Abu-Garcia Reels, 208
Accurate Reels, 210
aluminum, 5, 10, 11, 14, 17, 18, 21, 33, 196, 198
Aluminum, 15
anodized aluminum, 10, 11
Avet Reels, 212, 213

B

Bait Casting Reels, 8
Ball Bearings, 21, 22, 229
BALL BEARINGS, 9
Braided, 160, 165, 169, 172, 173
Breaking Strength, 167
bronze, 11, 14, 19, 22, 23
Bushings, 21

C

carbonite, 31
Carbontex, 153
cast control, 151, 152
CASTING CONTROLS, 10
centrifugal, 10
Ceramic Bearings, 27
Charles Frederick Holder, 3
Class lines, 168
Closed Face Spinning Reels, 8
Coils, 179
Conventional, 8, 27
Cryogenic, 194, 197, 198, 199

D

Dacron, 11, 159, 160
Daiwa, 18, 31, 42, 45, 147, 214
Diameter, 12, 26, 165, 169
drag, 3, 4, 6, 7, 9, 28, 30, 31, 32, 35, 43, 44, 150, 153, 154, 171, 172, 179, 186
drag system, 3, 7, 9, 30, 32
DRAG SYSTEMS, 9
DuPont, 159, 175
Durability, 176
Dyneema, 161

F

Fin-Nor Reels, 216
Flexibility, 16, 172
Fluorocarbon, 163, 164, 169, 177
Fly Reel, 8
Fuego, 18, 147
Fused Microfilament, 165

G

Gear Ratio, 12
GEAR RATIO, 9, 11
George Snyder, 2
graphite, 10, 11, 15, 22, 43, 46
Graphite, 10, 15, 40

H

Hardy Reels, 218
HOUSINGS AND FRAMES, 10

I

IGFA class, 168

J

James Vom Hofe, 4

K

Kentucky Reels, 2
Kevlar, 161, 166
Knot Strength, 172

L

LEVEL WIND MECHANISMS, 11
Line and Lure Conditioner, 187
LINE RECOVERY, 11
Line Twist, 179
Lubrication, 39, 42, 43, 45, 46, 47

M

Ma Yuan, 1
Magnesium, 17, 18
magnetic, 10
Meek, 2, 5, 6
microfilaments, 161, 165
Microfilaments, 171
Molybdenum Disulfide, 40
Monofilament, 159, 179, 197

O

Ocean City's, 31
Okuma, 31, 219
Open Faced Spinning Reels, 8

P

Penn, 6, 7, 31, 38, 222, 223
pinion, 19, 43, 151, 154, 201
Pinnacle Reels, 220
Plastics, 15, 16, 18
Polymer, 15, 22

Q

Quantum Reels, 224

R

ReelSchematic Chile Pepper Sauce, 37, 38
ReelSchematic Muscle Grease, 37, 38

S

Shakespeare, 227
Shimano Reels, 229
Spectra, 161, 165, 166
SPOOLS, 11
stainless steel, 5, 9, 11, 14, 15, 19, 23, 28, 29, 34, 35
Star drags, 9
Stretch, 165, 171
Super Slick, 32, 38, 39, 41
superlines, 161, 162, 164

T

Titanium, 15
Tungsten Disulfide, 39, 40, 41

U

Uniformity, 174

V

Viscosity, 39
Visibility, 175

W

WD-40, 187, 201
William C. Boschen, 7

worm shaft, 156

Z

Zebco Reels, 230

NOTES

Made in the USA
Charleston, SC
12 January 2010